TIMBER IN THE CITY

TIMBER IN THE CITY

DESIGN AND CONSTRUCTION IN MASS TIMBER

Edited by
Andrew Bernheimer
Essays by
Alan Organschi and Andrew Waugh

ORO EDITIONS

PARSONS THE NEW SCHOOL FOR DESIGN

Association of Collegiate Schools of Architecture
www.acsa-arch.org

BSLC
Binational Softwood Lumber Council

ORO EDITIONS
Publishers of Architecture, Art, and Design
Gordon Goff: Publisher
www.oroeditions.com
info@oroeditions.com

Published by ORO Editions

Consulting Editor: Andrea Monfried
Designer: Dungjai Pungauthaikan
Research Assistant: Gizem Sivri

10 9 8 7 6 5 4 3 First edition

Library of Congress Cataloging-in-Publication Data
Timber in the city : design and construction in mass timber / edited by Andrew Bernheimer ; essays by Alan Organschi and Andrew Waugh.
pages cm
ISBN 978-1-941806-80-7
1. Building, Wooden—New York (State)—Red Hook—Designs and plans. 2. Building, Wooden—Competitions.
3. Red Hook (New York, N.Y.)—Buildings, structures, etc.—Designs and plans. I. Organschi, Alan, author.
II. Waugh, Andrew (Architect), author. III. Bernheimer, Andrew, 1968- editor.
NA4110.T56 2015
721'.0448—dc23 2014038842

Color Separations and Printing: ORO Group Ltd.
Printed in China

International Distribution: www.oroeditions.com/distribution

CONTENTS

PREFACE

This book summarizes speculations on the present and future of our built environment. As synthetic materials and mutant and hybrid concoctions attain prominence in our daily lives—in our handheld devices, cooking utensils, vehicles, even things as simple as our shopping bags—the design and construction industries have instead reembraced the familiar, the conventional. Yet many of these materials have regained prominence through innovations in engineering and construction methodologies. Technology is now commonly used—and often (though not always) affordably used—to cut, perforate, assemble, erect, and even fabricate materials in a manner not previously possible. Wood is one such material, and this book documents both the imaginings of those in the nascence of their education and practice and the executed work of design professionals at the leading edge of architecture. These designers, regardless of the duration of their immersion in the field, have imaginatively rethought the means by which we build and the methods by which we define space merely through differing deployments of a familiar building material.

The catalyst for this book was the Timber in the City competition organized by the Association of Collegiate Schools of Architecture, the Binational Softwood Lumber Council, and Parsons The New School for Design. The competition sparked discussion about the manufacturing sector and modes of production related to mass timber. As a consequence we expanded the scope of this accompanying publication to include both essays, which enrich the database of work surrounding this important subject, and current works, which represent the present-day thinking of leading professionals worldwide.

In formulating the Timber in the City competition, the ACSA, BSLC, and Parsons aimed to stimulate material invention and broaden knowledge of contemporary timber technology. The competition brief posited a mixed-use facility containing manufacturing and affordable housing. In many cases entrants imagined a building that would construct itself; this modular growth would then foster an environment of modular living. The site, Red Hook, Brooklyn, is isolated from much of its borough but adjacent to New York Harbor. The area is undergoing gentrification yet is also at risk, exposed as it is to rising water levels and still recovering from the environmental cataclysm of Superstorm Sandy.

ACSA has coordinated many design competitions, but this was the first focused on wood technology and innovation. The subject could not be more timely: high-performance buildings have become far more common as a dedication by the best architects to research into material performance has become characteristic of the design process. Architects and engineers spend far more time gauging whether their designs can be implemented responsibly, locally, and renewably. In the best circumstances, an ethical approach to building materiality conjoins with aesthetic considerations. The best and most important buildings today are those that contemplate their impact on our resources and on our communities.

More than 200 entries from over 1,000 students and young professionals were submitted to the competition. The jurors—design professionals, teachers, and a developer—selected six projects notable for their use of mass timber in varying scales, their design excellence, and their representational invention, as well as their sensitivity to the New York City neighborhood for which they were designed and, more generally, to neighborhood-building in a modern city.

It is important for the responsible growth of our cities to consider innovations in traditional building materials. While as practitioners and educators we often tout the "brand new," emphasize the foreign or the unfamiliar, and love to speculate wildly about the potential of the amorphous unknown, we often find answers in extant, somewhat obvious materials and technologies. Wood is just one of these. Both in work being constructed around the world and in the entries to the competition, it is clear that while there is beautiful, inspiring, and technically innovative design ongoing, there simply isn't enough of it. Whether this is due to a lack of familiarity with newly available technologies, a fear of contemporary building systems, or even restrictive and long-lasting building codes (often based on outmoded risk factors), we must alter how we design and how we build.

The process of developing the competition and this book has been particularly important to me as an educator. It is essential that our schools and programs of architecture explore the technical and aesthetic potential of contemporary material technologies, including mass timber. At Parsons, both undergraduate and graduate studios have explored the pragmatic and poetic possibilities of wood to great impact on students and instructors alike. The students who have graduated into practice are prepared to grapple with a substance rich in texture, deep with strength. It is my hope that practitioners who engage this publication will likewise grasp the beautiful and innovative attributes of this natural material, consequently renewing their own architecture.

The book and the competition are the result of the hard work and contributions of many people. I offer my sincere thanks to those who have assisted with funding, coordination, and production. Cees de Jager of the Binational Softwood Lumber Council is a tireless and enthusiastic advocate for sustainability in construction and in particular for the importance of innovation in timber design. Bill Morrish, former dean of the School of Constructed Environments at Parsons The New School for Design, first hatched the concept of this program. David Lewis, interim dean of SCE during the 2012–13 academic year, offered pointed commentary and critique on the competition. Eric Ellis, director of operations and programs at the Association of Collegiate Schools of Architecture, coordinated the competition through countless stages, from inception through final jury. Pascale Vonier and Angela DeGeorge, also of ACSA, worked on the original competition. Alfred Zollinger, at the School of Constructed Environments, offered advice and insights while the competition was in formation; Zollinger, along with Lewis and Alan Bruton, has led studios that have focused on the possibilities and implementation of mass timber designs. Oni Lloyd and Andrew McGregor, graduates of the Parsons M.Arch. program, researched site and program during the initial drafting of the competition. Emmanuel Oni, also a graduate, assisted with events surrounding the installation of a show at Parsons about the competition.

I am also grateful to those who played a role in the physical and intellectual crafting of this book. Alan Organschi and Andrew Waugh, two of the competition jurors, have contributed writings and projects to the publication; their creativity and intellect will surely be the basis for deep research by many other talented architects. Gizem Sivri, a graduate of the M.Arch. program at Parsons, assisted with the production. Dungjai Pungauthaikan created a design that is at once clever and highly refined. Last, Andrea Monfried pulled together the numerous participants and crafted a cohesive structure for the publication. Without her efforts this would not have happened.

Andrew Bernheimer
Assistant Professor, Director of the Master of Architecture Program
Parsons The New School for Design
School of Constructed Environments

ESSAYS

ESSAY

Timber City: Architectural Speculations in a Black Market

Alan Organschi

Economics is the science which studies human behaviour as a relationship between ends and scarce means which have alternative uses.

—**Lionel Robbins**, *An Essay on the Nature and Significance of Economic Science*

Without resources there can be no economic activity. I call this the physical conception of economics: all economic activity consists in essence of converting materials in their raw state into finished products using converted energy; this includes the energy for communication, consumption, transport and distribution. In essence the economic process is first and foremost a process of converting resources. But it matters very much—not solely for ecological reasons—what resources we use and how we use them.

—**Hermann Scheer**, "Solar City: Reconnecting *Energy Generation and Use to the Technical and Social Logic of Solar Energy*"

If humanity wishes to preserve a planet similar to that on which civilization developed and to which life on Earth is adapted, paleoclimate evidence and ongoing climate change suggest that CO_2 will need to be reduced from its current 385 ppm to at most 350 ppm ... The largest uncertainty in the target arises from possible changes of non-CO_2 forcings. An initial 350 ppm CO_2 target may be achievable by phasing out coal use except where CO_2 is captured and adopting agricultural and forestry practices that sequester carbon. If the present overshoot of this target CO_2 is not brief, there is a possibility of seeding irreversible catastrophic effects.

—**James Hansen et al.**, "Target Atmospheric CO_2: *Where Should Humanity Aim?*"

We're trying to figure out how to make carbon an asset.

—**Klaus Töpfer**, Cities and Climate Change Network *Conference, Potsdam, 2012*

Consider this building material: a complex carbohydrate, synthesized biologically using solar energy and carbon dioxide, with an exceptionally high strength-to-weight ratio. The fibrous substance is formed by the annual introduction of tiny capsules containing a complex but naturally occurring arrangement of nucleic acids to the earth's soils and the regular recharging of that surface with rainwater and sunlight. A single capsule, costing nothing to produce or to distribute, is usually a little less than a centimeter in length and, depending on atmospheric, hydrologic, and soil conditions, can generate more than a metric ton of structural material in a little over 50 years. The supply is potentially infinite, and where extraction is well-managed, the landscapes that are its source will naturally and rapidly regenerate, providing critical environmental services such as well-oxygenated air, filtered potable water, and an array of marketable consumer products, all while protecting diverse biological habitats and sequestering significant amounts of atmospheric carbon. The energies required for its processing are low compared to other common structural materials. Residues left over from the material extraction process can be left as a kind of nutritive feedstock for future production, contributing either to increasingly compressed layers of carbon-rich soil or to a sustainable exchange of aerobic decay and carbon uptake. Similarly, processing waste serves as fuel for the manufacture of building products.

The material is readily available globally, and the landscapes from which it is extracted happen to fall in relative proximity to many major cities, reducing transport energies and emissions. Various forms of its fiber can be used in an array of commercial building products: structural members with a range of capacities and applications, highly insulated and thermally broken wall and roof assemblies, and durable interior surfaces able to regulate swings in interior moisture levels. The material is lightweight and easily worked, making its initial construction, its repair, and its dismantling and re- or upcycling less technologically intensive. The material is applicable to all but a few of the building types and civil infrastructural components common to dense urban aggregations. When applied and detailed properly within a building enclosure, the material is extremely durable, and—most critically at this particular global moment—the carbon absorbed during its synthesis remains embedded in its molecular structure as long as the building is maintained or until its assemblies break down and the material decays or, more catastrophically, burns.

If it weren't so patently obvious that I've just described wood, forests, and photosynthesis, this passage might read like an elevator pitch for a geo-engineering start-up or a book jacket for an eco-utopian novel. Instead I hope to frame a simple argument for a potential (and rapidly realizable) ecological and economic synergy between two landscapes, the forest and the city, as they function symbiotically to absorb and store atmospheric carbon. What I propose is the transformation of our cities from CO_2 source to carbon sink through the development of new urban structural typologies in wood: a timber city.

Our current culture of land use and resource allocation, and the regulatory systems that reinforce it, tends to direct timber away from our cities. Historic concerns about the overuse of wood and the resulting destruction of forests, misgivings and misapprehensions about the properties and vulnerabilities of structural timber, and deeply embedded cultural associations with wood as a provisional service material with a relatively low structural capacity have combined to relegate contemporary use of timber to the commercially profitable but relatively modest structural demands of light-framed, low-rise, low-density applications in the residential building sector. On a continent as timber rich as North America, it is both a conceptual irony and a significant environmental risk that this renewable material, with demonstrably low extraction, processing, and production impacts and energy demands, has given rise to the land- and energy-intensive sprawl of suburbia, one of the United States' most durable and pervasive global exports. Meanwhile, the materially demanding building morphologies of our cities, with their relatively efficient use of surface area, space, and infrastructure, are generated from a class of structural materials with a large carbon footprint.

That the very way we go about constructing our built environment, currently a significant source of overall anthropogenic greenhouse gas emissions, might instead be recognized as a means to *offset* them, is a compelling concept, one supported by recent research on building life cycle impacts and forest-carbon management, bolstered by rapid breakthroughs in mass timber engineering and production technology, and made all the more pressing by mounting evidence of rapidly accelerating global climate change. At this particular moment, however, when fossil fuels with high energy densities—coal, oil, and most recently, natural gas—remain abundant and cheap, building-material industries that rely on them will continue to produce high-strength, high-impact products like steel and concrete at relatively low financial cost. Under these circumstances, an economic value proposition about the affordability of mass timber construction is difficult to make. Professional architecture and engineering practice, the commercial building industry, and real estate development culture continue to operate within a strict system of financial analysis, bounded by a relatively short time frame for monetary investment and return. When carbon emissions and their impacts become monetized, however, through various regulatory regimes or economic devices like a carbon tax or cap-and-trade schemes, the boundaries of that cost analysis expand. In an economic system in which emissions reductions are endowed with financial value, the conceptual and material shift of cities from anthropogenic source of greenhouse gas to human-made carbon storage system becomes an appealing proposition. What small city, struggling with budget deficits, wouldn't gladly reap the financial benefits of a sale of carbon credits to an industrial polluter seeking emissions offsets?

This speculation has both temporal and spatial dimensions. The time frame of accelerating climate change, expressed as a projected increase in the atmospheric concentration of carbon dioxide and its greenhouse gas equivalents, has already surpassed thresholds anticipated only a few years ago as being decades away. Analytic predictions that incorporate existing climate forcings, that is, impacts of past human activity with warming potential already in the pipeline, give humankind only a few decades to make dramatic reductions in anthropogenic emissions or seek significant means of offsetting the current emissions rate before reaching a tipping point.[1] Little time separates us, in a scenario of continuing increases in atmospheric CO_2, from "irreversible catastrophic" effects.[2] This means that any effort to reduce our impacts in the building sector, a significant contributor of greenhouse gas, must yield near-immediate results.

The classes of structural material that catalyzed urban construction during the late nineteenth- and twentieth-century expansion of the industrial city and that today continue to be applied as commercial and professional reflex are primarily mineral-based and energy-demanding. The high-reaching, long-spanning, heavy-load-bearing urban artifacts constructed from iron, steel, and concrete (and sheathed in increasingly uninterrupted expanses of aluminum, glass, and plastic composites) were smelted, sintered, and synthesized from raw materials extracted from subsurface geological strata through extensive land-degrading mining. Their processing and production energy demands were satisfied with hydrocarbons drawn from an ever-deeper cross section of the earth's crust with increasingly intensified extraction technologies (fig. 1). Industrial fuel, first gathered from dense plant matter from the biosphere (forests) and then excavated from seams of geologically compacted hydrocarbons in the upper lithosphere (coal), is today drawn from deep reserves through energy- and technology-intensive (and dangerously invasive) extraction (fossil oil and gas). In the more efficient margins of this heavy industry sector, there have been significant improvements in resource productivity through changes in feedstocks and material recycling. Technology upgrades have resulted in energy efficiencies and associated reductions in greenhouse gas emissions.[3] But for the bulk of global cement and steel manufacturers, especially in rapidly developing and urbanizing countries where demands for structural materials capable of higher-density and higher-rise building applications are climbing, the transformation of manufacturing technologies may be too slow in coming. The oxygen furnace and the sintering of Portland cement may linger as means and processes with dangerous impacts.[4]

An immediate spike in building industry emissions may be the unintentional result of the current efforts to reduce our impacts.[5] Our relatively recent efforts to recalibrate and refine building envelopes and mechanical systems in search of any and all potential operational efficiencies have been critical exercises that will yield, over time, some long-term savings in fossil energy consumption and CO_2 emissions. But anyone who has studied the building life cycle recognizes that the front-loading of emissions embodied in the production of technologically intensive, high-performance building materials and assemblies will take decades—and in the most energy-efficient buildings as much as building lifetime—to offset.[6] And as global temperatures rise, cooling loads will rise too; increased demands on enclosure assemblies and mechanical systems in summer months may effectively erase the benefits of performance upgrades[7] and leave their initial ecological costs (measured in embodied emissions) unrecovered. In any currency—dollars, euros, renminbi, or carbon emissions—return rates on investments are expected to keep ahead of inflation. And in our current condition, characterized by an inflationary trend in CO_2 emissions that we are hoping desperately to arrest, the econometric significance of environmental *first* costs and impacts of embodied emissions is far greater than their minority share of overall building life cycle emissions might suggest. A compounding factor in this time-sensitive economic equation is that many of the materials essential to the technical systems that have made our recent buildings perform so well have entailed, in their extraction and manufacture, the intensive

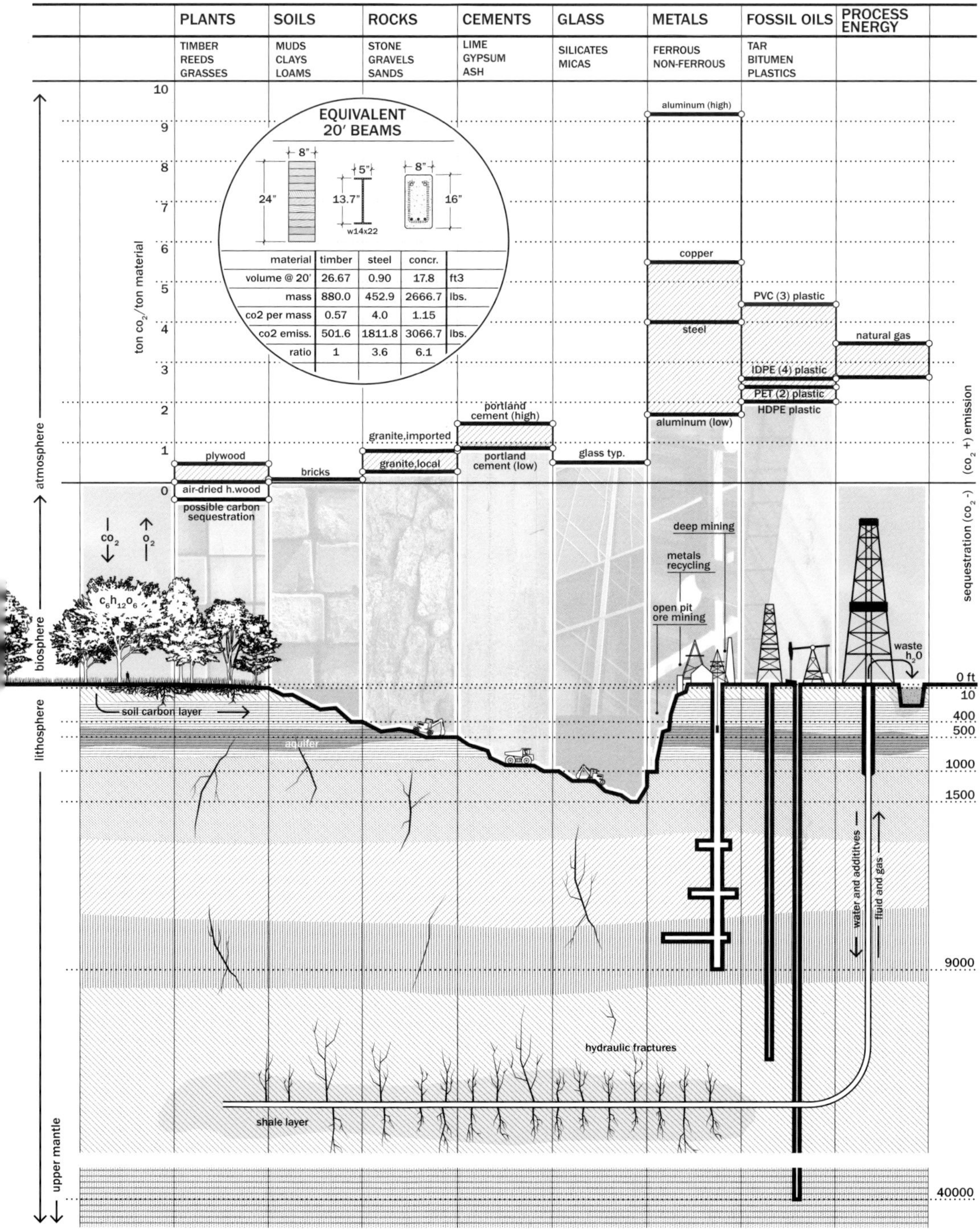

material	timber	steel	concr.	
volume @ 20'	26.67	0.90	17.8	ft3
mass	880.0	452.9	2666.7	lbs.
co2 per mass	0.57	4.0	1.15	
co2 emiss.	501.6	1811.8	3066.7	lbs.
ratio	1	3.6	6.1	

use of petrochemicals (either as an energy source or a synthetic component), enlarging their carbon footprints significantly as compared to poorer-performing alternatives.[8]

The spatial dimension of this argument is measured at two scales: that of the land area we disrupt in building human settlement and that of the volume of building material we call upon to do it. The benefits compound each other when we build dense cities using dense structural formations of timber to produce familiar mid-rise building morphologies and uses: the sequestration of approximately 1.6 metric tons of atmospheric CO_2 in each ton of timber utilized and maintained in buildings[9]; the uptake of CO_2 in the replacement of forest stocks over a 40-to-60-year growth cycle; the avoidance of fossil fuel emissions embodied in the manufacture of alternative, mineral-based structural products.[10] We must add to this complex but critical calculus of material expenditure and carbon emissions the important factor of potential energy savings and impact reduction that we capture by redirecting resources away from the production of attenuated suburban infrastructural systems with their energy-gobbling and heat-absorbing networks of roads and parking lots; their overtaxed, rickety, and electrically leaky power grids; and their forest-fragmenting, land-degrading organizations of buildings.[11] These benefits and offsets exploit global demographic shifts in population and wealth to cities that are already underway[12] and redirect the consumption of new building materials that will inevitably result.

As a brief thought experiment, consider the savings (with interest!) that would accrue in reconfiguring the structural components of what was once central to the American Dream: the studs, joists, rafters, and plywood sheathing and subfloors of an average 2,400-square-foot, single-family suburban house. If the wood fiber contained in the 38,000 board feet (30 metric tons) of light sticks and thin veneers that form the skeletal system of suburbia were instead laid up as dense, structurally efficient glue-laminated assemblies to produce equivalently sized, similarly programmed units of mid-rise urban housing, we would shift approximately 1,500 households onto an area of land that would hold only about 30 families in freestanding wood-framed suburban houses (fig. 2). The costs of producing better-performing building envelopes and mechanical systems would be shared by many, relieving the individual homeowner of the increasingly onerous demands of maintaining a freestanding high-performance home.[13] Mass timber, previously underutilized in the heavy-bearing structures associated with urban dwelling and the cityscape, might now be embedded in parking garages, bridges and overpasses, commercial buildings, and industrial facilities, storing carbon reserves in a symbiotic offset of the carbon emitted by the drivers and cars that use them (fig. 3). The land area left undisturbed by exodus to suburbia, potentially freed of its modestly diffuse, yet physically burdensome population, unencumbered by impermeable soil cover, and increasingly diversified biologically with hydrological systems intact, is now a biomass producer and high-functioning collector of CO_2. Carbon is a structural asset, the dense urban center its parsimonious bank.

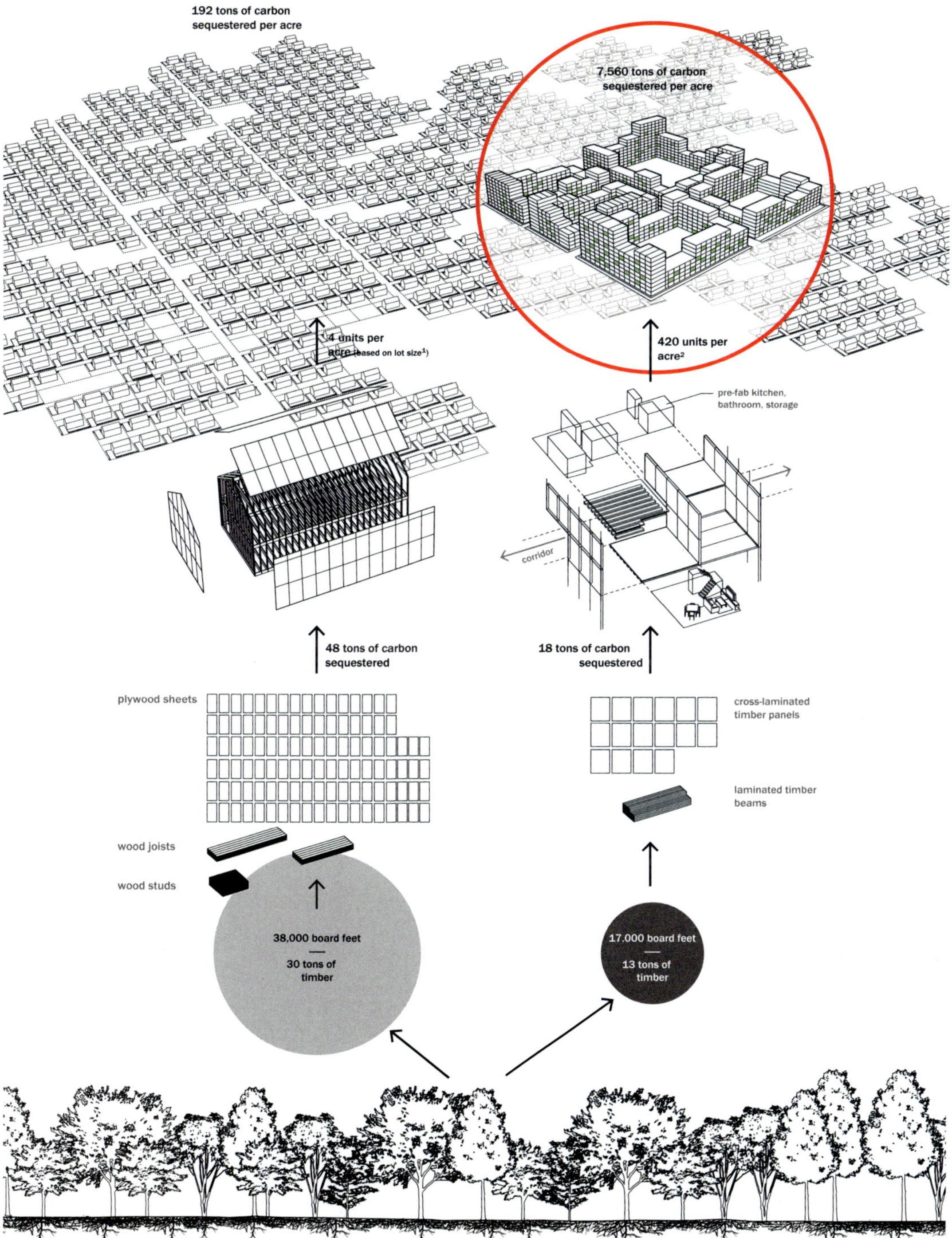
192 tons of carbon sequestered per acre
7,560 tons of carbon sequestered per acre
4 units per acre (based on lot size[1])
420 units per acre[2]
pre-fab kitchen, bathroom, storage
corridor
48 tons of carbon sequestered
18 tons of carbon sequestered
plywood sheets
cross-laminated timber panels
laminated timber beams
wood joists
wood studs
38,000 board feet — 30 tons of timber
17,000 board feet — 13 tons of timber

CROSS-LAMINATED TIMBER

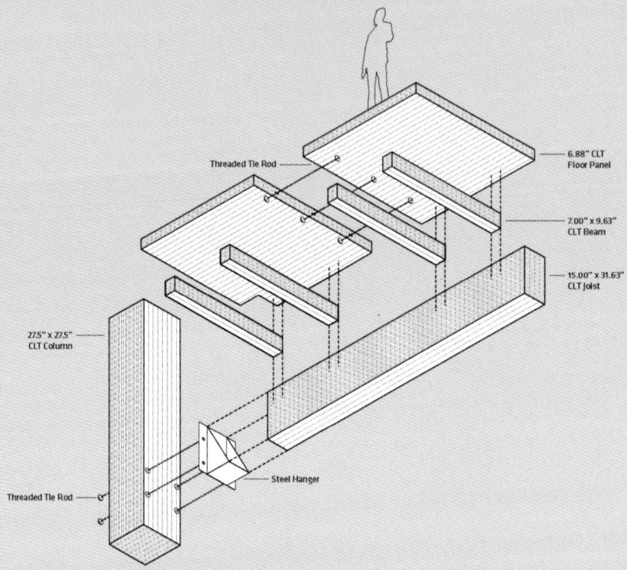

A PREFAB SYSTEM FOR PARKING IN THE 21ST CENTURY

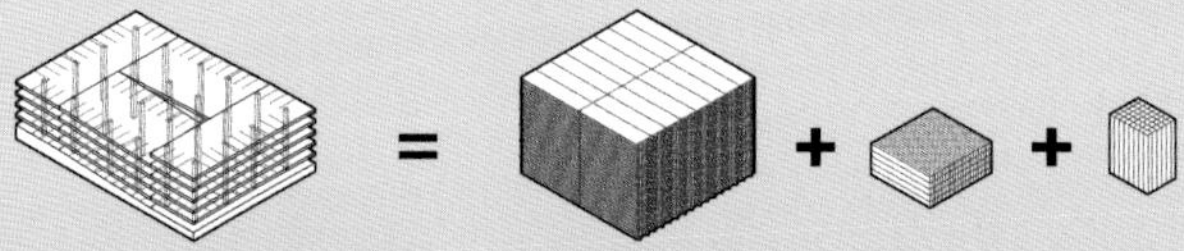

= 86,000 ft^3 Cross-Laminated Timber
= 2,500,000 kg CO_2 sequestered

vs. concrete base case

Carbon Savings Equivalent to

18 MONTHS

of Emissions-Free Driving!!!

for all 320 cars using the garage

Redeploying material and reorganizing land at these scales might be easily dismissed as unworkable fantasy. But considered more thoroughly and developed econometrically, this structural argument starts to bear real loads. The accounting anticipates inevitably massive investment in the material and technology required to house shifting populations in necessarily better-performing building envelopes. It incorporates the findings of current research and experimentation in silviculture[14] and building production. It assigns value to an economic symbiosis found in forest supply and construction demand, which has both environmental implications and immediate application around the globe. Well-argued speculations in wooden "skyscraper" engineering[15] have served as exciting provocations. But less height-ambitious versions, six- to twelve-story mid-rise, mixed-use timber buildings completed or under construction in London, Finland, Austria, Germany, Canada, and Australia, along with heavy timber vehicular bridges in Canada and the Netherlands and a timber parking garage in Sweden, are all the proof needed to pursue the development of the cityscapes imagined here. And the carbon benefits are quantifiable and easily projected across larger urban developments with greater economies of scale.

For a range of reasons, old (in some cases, ancient) yet still evolving tectonic procedures of stacking, bundling, through-bolted assembly, and more recently glue laminating failed to catalyze a manufacturing revolution in mass timber construction during the last century of rapid building expansion. But today, they are beginning to reveal wood's secrets and yield potential solutions to architects, planners, and policy makers searching for sustainable yet durable building systems. The very material properties of wood and structural timber that have made its performance in building difficult to predict and therefore resistant to industrial standardization are now proving, when understood, exploited, and properly applied, to be great assets with significant collateral benefits. Qualities of structural wood long held to be potential liabilities—its low density, combustibility, complex anisotropic strength characteristics, constant hygroscopic absorption of moisture—are proving through new research and product development to be sustainable technological assets.

It is perhaps wood's natural heterogeneity, the unpredictable defects of the raw material, and the variation in the properties, processing requirements, and performance characteristics of the fiber (depending on species and growing region) that have been timber's greatest disadvantage in the marketplace of high-strength structural products. The varying properties of different species drawn from the same forest and even the differing structural capacity of timber sawn from the same tree have been a disincentive to a building industry seeking economies of scale, repetitive manufacturing procedures, and homogenous raw material. But analytical protocols and industrial practices that are already in place at a basic level in mass timber manufacturing may provide the seeds for a more tolerant and holistic use of the structural materials available in the forest.

Ingrained in the technological processes of timber glue lamination—whether for a piece of engineered flooring or a massive structural panel—

is a set of well-established procedural steps designed to eliminate defects, catalog the wood fiber based on quality and structural capacity, and distribute it efficiently within a structural member. The sorting, grading, and re-sawing, the removal of flaws (unsound knots or checks), and the subsequent finger-jointing of small boards into longer, structurally improved sticks allow the strongest and highest-quality material found in a tree to be positioned where it can do the most structural work. Current standard practice in the industrial layup of a glue-laminated beam, for example, places the higher-grade laminations at the more structurally critical tension and compression edges of the member; the weaker, lower-quality fibers fall in the less demanding midsection.

Digital analysis and material optimization systems that are increasingly industry standards can produce enormous efficiencies in the use of the trees we cut. They also create the potential for a more comprehensive approach to our forests as a renewable resource, optimizing the use of a range of species with lower structural values, that in turn enables us to manage forest stands in ways that better emulate natural growth. The current insatiable commercial demand for the perfect piece of wood—whatever the preference, be it straight, stable, rot-resistant, beautifully figured, behaviorally predictable—has promoted the predatory practice of culling only certain commercially "hot" or well-known species from global forests, or plucking the finest, most recognizably profitable trees from a particular stand, while leaving lesser-known and commercially underutilized trees and thereby distorting the ecological balances of the forest. Timber plantations, which often favor monocultures over more ecologically diverse forests with natural growth through a succession of species, have proven profitable in some cases but, with the wrong microclimate or soil type, have led to erosion and soil degradation while producing wood of decreasing quality.[16]

By developing an array of structural products and assemblies that seek to exploit existing techniques in mass timber production and to utilize a greater diversity of plant fiber growing naturally in our forests, we can promote healthy silvicultural diversity while fixing increasing amounts of carbon in the structural products we specify. Recent experimentation anticipates the broader use of mixed-species layups; these distribute woods with different properties within customized configurations designed for varying structural demands and applications. New products already in the pipeline include hybridized structural members and assemblies that take advantage of the lightness, appearance, renewability, or tensile strength of timber while introducing small, optimally configured amounts of glass and carbon fiber, steel, or reinforced concrete to magnify performance.[17] Today our use of structural timber is limited to a narrow spectrum of commercially familiar species and grades of solid lumber. The processes inherent in mass timber technologies might offer a promising means to broaden our use of this abundant resource. In the United States, we have only begun to develop new mass timber systems as commercial products; teach their principles, means, methods, and potentialities in our design and engineering schools; measure and articulate their environmental benefits; and adopt their solutions in the professional arena.

For those with justifiable anxiety about the 15 to 20 percent of global deforestation directly attributable to the harvested wood products industry, who might recoil at the prospect of the mass destruction of the planet's forests in our zeal to craft new cities from wood, it is important to acknowledge historic abuses and potential mismanagement. The economics of our past destructiveness—the undervaluing and misapplication of certain wood species and products, the simplistic and inefficient uses of their fiber, and the rather crude exploitation of forests as an unregulated and infinite source of profit—all contributed to historic damage and degradation. But the intense and imbalanced market demands that sponsored those predatory practices are now giving way to promising techniques that seek economic advantage in wood's broad applicability and renewability, rather than its mere homogeneity, and that reflect the sophistication and nuance of our current understanding of forest stand dynamics.[18] The challenge today is a system-wide accounting that seeks to balance the potential productivity of forest ecologies in relation to the material and energy demands of the construction sector. The solution lies in a mix of approaches to the preservation of historically diverse forests and the expansion and utilization of new forest land by developing sustainable material and economic demands for its wood and exploiting its processes of carbon uptake and storage.[19]

Although architects, engineers, policy makers, and builders tend to think of themselves as producers, as *makers* of the built environment, we are, in fact, mass consumers. And like all consumers who draw directly or indirectly on often finite supplies of material and call up complex, technologically intensive processes in our demand for goods, we have an embodied energy and emissions problem.[20] Through professional reflex, commercial convention, or cultural habit, we pull hard on the demand end of a complex economic chain without completely understanding or assessing the actual environmental (and inevitably socioeconomic) predations and impacts of what it supplies.

In doing so, we speculate with considerable risk in a black market: *black* in the metaphorical sense because the building systems we call into being and the complicated processes of producing them contribute each year to a significant uptick in the amount of carbon introduced into the atmosphere by human activity; a *black market* because we conduct a constant and complex exchange of material and energy that is unregulated and crudely measured. As professionals, we *speculate* in this black economy by making risky transactions on a daily basis, calling upon enormous physical resources with promises of significant profits in energy efficiency, impact reduction, and renewability. The econometrics are tricky and highly contested; the techniques of carbon cost-benefit analysis are clumsy and subject to conflicts of interest and undue influence. The boundaries of the systems we can reliably assess are so narrow, the mechanism of exchange so far-reaching, the infrastructure of resource extraction, processing, delivery so pervasive, and the cycles of carbon uptake and release so immediate—a photon striking a leaf's chlorophyll, the sudden firing of a basement boiler, the pulsation of refrigerant pumps—and yet so global in dimension and so geologic in duration that our claims for the performance of our buildings and the impacts of their manufacture are, at best, constantly changing and, at worst, woefully inadequate or even willfully misleading.

In the physical economics of converting raw material into the finished product of building, we will ultimately account for what Lionel Robbins described as "a relationship between ends and scarce means." In seeking his potential "alternative uses" in an exchange already taking place at a global scale, it would be grandiose to suggest that the sole solution to pending planetary crisis is the adoption of mass timber in the construction of new, densely built environments. But as the window for climate action narrows and shifting urban demographics create new demands for physical resources, it seems obvious that the carbon held both in forests and, potentially, in an array of urban buildings is an asset we should develop and manage.

Alan Organschi is a design principal and a partner at Gray Organschi Architecture in New Haven, Connecticut. He is also a lecturer at the Yale School of Architecture and coordinates Yale's first-year graduate housing studio. Organschi has lectured on architecture, technology, and the ecological impacts of design at universities and public and professional forums in the United States, Canada, and Europe.

1. James Hansen et al., "Target Atmospheric CO_2: Where Should Humanity Aim?" *Open Atmospheric Science Journal* 2 (2008): 217.

2. Hansen, "Target Atmospheric CO_2," 217.

3. Ernst von Weizsäcker et al., *Factor Five: Transforming the Global Economy Through 80 Percent Improvements in Resource Productivity* (London: Earthscan, 2009), 143–70.

4. Weizsäcker, *Factor Five*, 51.

5. Miro Ristimäki et al., "Combining Life Cycle Costing and Life Cycle Assessment for an Analysis of a New Residential District Energy System," *Energy* 63 (2013): 168–79.

6. I. Sartori and A. G. Hestnes, "Energy Use in the Life Cycle of Conventional and Low-Energy Buildings: A Review Article," *Energy and Buildings* 39, no. 3 (2007): 249–57; Ristimäki, "Combining Life Cycle Costing," 168–79; Vikas Khanna, Bhavik R. Bakshi, and L. James Lee, "Carbon Nanofiber Production: Life Cycle Energy Consumption and Environmental Impact," *Journal of Industrial Ecology* 12, no. 3 (2008): 394–410.

7. Zhengen Ren, Xiaoming Wang, and Dong Chen, "Climate Change Impacts on Housing Energy Consumption and Its Adaptation Pathways," in *Mitigating Climate Change: The Emerging Face of Modern Cities*, ed. Anshuman Khare and Terry Beckman (Berlin: Springer, 2013), 207–22.

8. Jennifer O'Connor and Jim Dangerfield, "The Environmental Benefits of Wood Construction" (paper delivered at Eighth World Conference on Timber Engineering, Lahti, Finland, 2004), 171–77.

9. Dominique Gauzin-Müller, ed., *Sustainable Architecture and Urbanism: Concepts, Technologies, Examples* (Basel: Birkhauser, 2002), 32–43.

10. Chadwick Dearing Oliver et al., "Carbon, Fossil Fuel, and Biodiversity Mitigation with Wood and Forests," *Journal of Sustainable Forestry* 33, no. 3 (2014): 248–75.

11. Eero Puurunen and Alan Organschi, "Multiplier Effect: High Performance Construction Assemblies and Urban Density in US Housing," in Khare and Beckman, *Mitigating Climate Change*, 183–206.

12. Barney Cohen, "Urbanization in Developing Countries: Current Trends, Future Projections, and Key Challenges for Sustainability," *Technology in Society* 28, no. 2 (2006): 63–80; Karen C. Seto, Burak Güneralp, and Lucy R. Hutyra, "Global Forecasts of Urban Expansion to 2030 and Direct Impacts on Biodiversity and Carbon Pools," *Proceedings of the National Academy of Sciences of the United States of America* 109, no. 40 (2012): 16083–88.

13. Puurunen and Organschi, "Multiplier Effect," 183–206.

14. Oliver et al., "Carbon, Fossil Fuel," 248–75.

15. Michael Green and J. Eric Karsh, "The Case for Tall Wood Buildings: How Mass Timber Offers a Safe, Economical, and Environmentally Friendly Alternative for Tall Building Structures," http://cwc.ca/wp-content/uploads/publications-Tall-Wood.pdf (Vancouver: mgb Architecture + Design et al., 2012), accessed August 4, 2014; Barbara Porada, "The Timber Tower Research Project: Re-Imagining the Skyscraper," *Arch Daily*, June 6, 2013, http://www.archdaily.com/384032/the-timber-tower-research-project-re-imagining-the-skyscraper, accessed August 4, 2014.

16. Chadwick Dearing Oliver and Roger Mesznik, "Investing in Forestry: Opportunities and Pitfalls of Intensive Plantations and Other Alternatives," *Journal of Sustainable Forestry* 21, no. 4 (2005): 97–111.

17. Nikolaos Plevris and Thanasis C. Triantafillou, "FRP-Reinforced Wood as Structural Material," *Journal of Materials in Civil Engineering* 4, no. 3 (1992): 300–317; Juliano Fiorelli and Antonio Alves Dias, "Analysis of the Strength and Stiffness of Timber Beams Reinforced with Carbon Fiber and Glass Fiber," *Materials Research* 6, no. 2 (2003): 193–202.

18. Chadwick D. Oliver and Bruce C. Larson, *Forest Stand Dynamics* (New York: John Wiley and Sons, 1996).

19. Oliver et al., "Carbon, Fossil Fuel," 248–75.

20. Manfred Lenzen, Richard Wood, and Barney Foran, "Direct versus Embodied Energy: The Need for Urban Lifestyle Transitions," in *Urban Energy Transition: From Fossil Fuels to Renewable Power*, ed. Peter Droege (Oxford: Elsevier, 2008), 91–120.

ESSAY

Twenty-First-Century Timber

Andrew Waugh

Architects today cannot afford to follow old models of design and construction. Two major issues—human-made climate change and a soaring world population—demand a new outlook. To accommodate future generations, whether in housing, at university, or in the workplace—we must reinvent construction with an eye to limited impact on our environment.

Approximately half of carbon emissions in the United Kingdom originate from the construction or use of buildings. The industry has for some time focused on "low-carbon" and "zero-carbon" projects, though these terms reflect only operational carbon—the heating, lighting, and ventilation of buildings. Emissions attributed to the production of construction materials and the process of construction are known as the embodied carbon—and these emissions are typically not included when the low- or no-carbon calculation is made. As energy regulation, standards, and efficiency increase, the embodied carbon of the building structure becomes proportionally greater, generating about half of the carbon emissions of a building over its lifetime.

A sizable contribution to carbon emissions comes from concrete, the dominant material in construction around the world. Manufacture of the cement that binds concrete is one of the industry's most polluting processes—every ton of cement produces a ton of carbon dioxide. In ongoing research into the principles of sustainability in construction, our office has turned to timber.

Timber is one of the world's oldest building materials; more to the point, it soaks up carbon dioxide as it grows. A cubic meter of engineered timber can remove up to a ton of carbon dioxide from the atmosphere, storing the carbon and releasing the oxygen. The more timber we use, the better it is for the environment.

Modern engineered timber is a sophisticated construction material, a material with immense structural capacity—pound for pound, it is four times stronger than steel. Buildings in timber rise quickly and accurately. Timber takes well to fasteners and is easy to adapt. Timber buildings are wonderful to live in, with an inherent humanity and a natural regulation of moisture and humidity. Sounds are softer and temperatures more comfortable.

Although wood construction, whether traditional or in mass timber, is readily accepted outside of urban areas, it is precisely in cities that it will have the most significant impact, in the present day and in the future. More than half of the Earth's population lives in cities; by 2050, the figure may rise to 70 percent. It is vital that the architecture and construction industries look to new tall timber structures in the building and rebuilding of healthy and humane cities.

Waugh Thistleton constructed our first—and the UK's first—cross-laminated timber building in 2004. The modest three-story building in Exton Street, South London, was conceived to capitalize on newly introduced legislation that sought to recognize and reduce the impact of construction on the environment. The use of engineered timber and CLT was an epiphany. Engineered wood is a superb building material—fast, exact, solid—and is unparalleled as a carbon store. The small structure, its natural beauty immediately apparent, flew up from the back of a single truck on a Saturday afternoon.

Murray Grove

Our next timber building was Murray Grove, a nine-story residential building in East London, in 2009. Between 2004 and 2009, we had continued to research solid timber, particularly with a view to high-density housing. The building was conceived as a model for future city living, one that demonstrates that timber is a viable alternative to concrete and steel in high-rise construction.

From the first floor up, Murray Grove is constructed entirely of timber; in fact, it is the first high-density, high-rise housing in the world to be built completely from CLT panels. (The client nicknamed the building Stadthaus in honor of the timber's Austrian origins.) Load-bearing walls and floor slabs are timber, but also stair and elevator cores. Structurally, the walls and floor slabs work together as a honeycomb. Short spans allow relatively slim panels to work in concert to provide a strong structure. The CLT panels act in three dimensions, their strength and stability a result of a close network of four- to six-inch-thick panels and standard fittings (four-inch galvanized angle brackets).

Designing a building from solid load-bearing panels offers opportunities to vary the internal layout from floor to floor: any internal wall can become a party wall, even with significant portions removed for openings. In the case of Murray Grove, the different interior plans generate an animated facade, with windows placed to suit specific room dispositions rather than aligned from floor to floor.

The building of Stadthaus was something to behold. Panels swung into place effortlessly, slotting together with rabbeted joints. Two workers harnessed to each completed floor slab guided precisely manufactured panels into a three-dimensional jigsaw puzzle that evolved day by day. The structure was completed in just twenty-seven days, and the entire project within a year; we estimate that a similar concrete structure would have taken eighteen months.

Material Qualities

Murray Grove, like Exton Street five years earlier, taught us much about both timber as a building material and timber construction as a potential solution to the environmental impacts of the construction industry. Timber is a beautiful natural substance; it is replenishable and, if left untreated, can be recycled. Heating and cooling the interior spaces takes much less

MURRAY GROVE
LONDON, ENGLAND
2009

PLAN

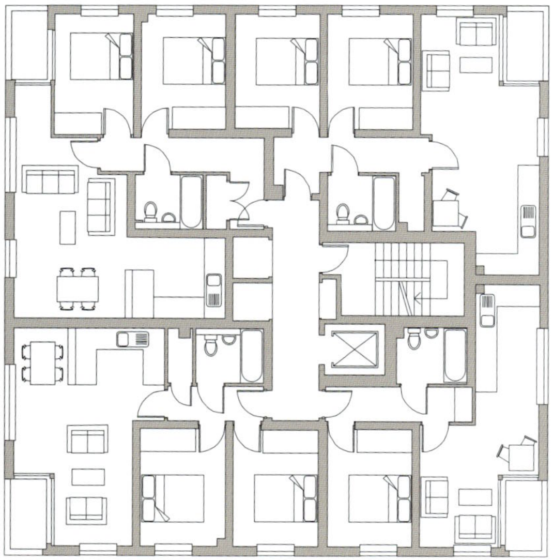

CUTAWAY SECTION

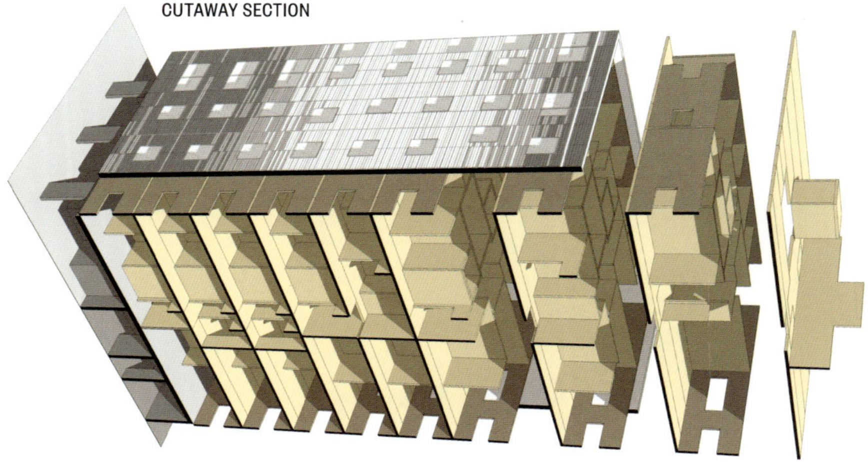

HEAD AND SILL DETAIL

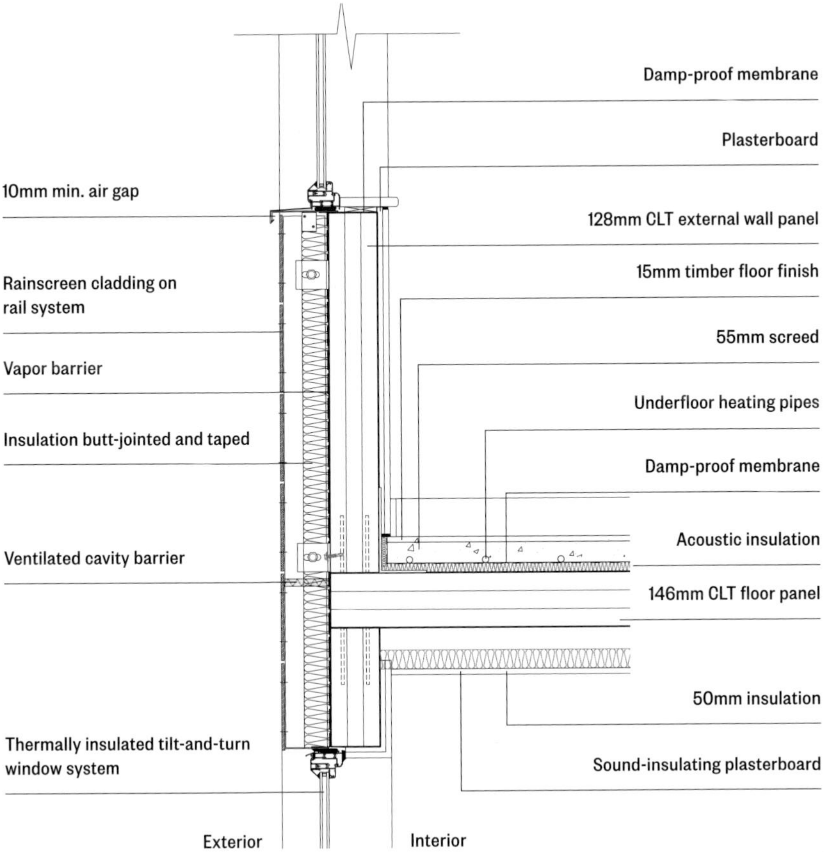

SEPARATING WALL/FLOOR VERTICAL SECTION

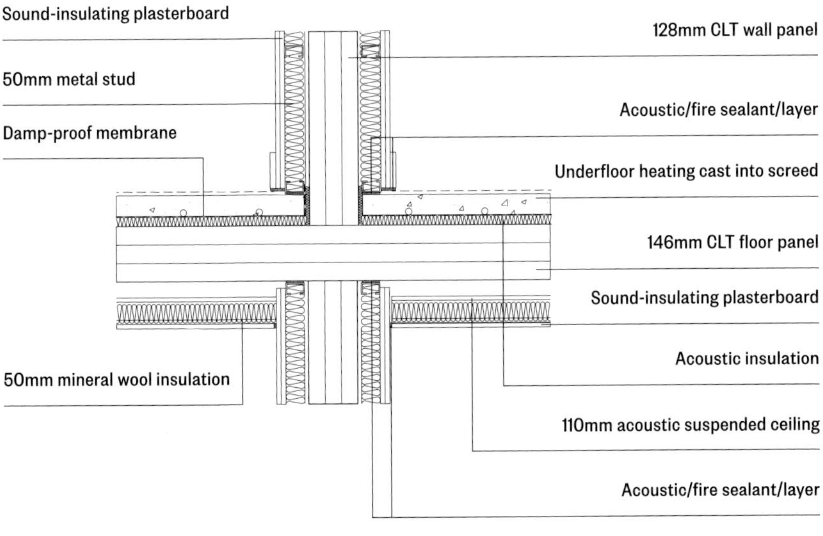

energy than would those of a masonry or concrete building because the slower thermal dynamic of timber maintains a far more even temperature.

Contractors and clients alike have expressed concern about the acoustic quality of timber buildings, in part because timber-frame buildings are classified as poor in comparison to reinforced concrete and masonry. Solid timber panels, however, are significantly higher in density than timber-frame buildings and must be considered in an entirely new light. They provide a solid structural core to which independent and separate layers can be added to overcome sound transfer. Floating floor build-ups and suspended ceilings furnish sound attenuation far in excess of code requirements.

Protection from fire is an analogous issue, though likewise unfounded. Solid timber meets and generally exceeds fire requirements. A steel frame might buckle after an hour; a solid timber structure forms a protective char layer on the surface and retains its structural integrity over greater lengths of time.

Cost is another frequent question with respect to solid timber construction. While the initial capital outlay for this new technology can be more than that for a traditional concrete and steel frame, significant savings are often realized on site. Timber requires shallower foundations and a shorter construction schedule; in addition, it is easier for the trades to finish the walls and soffit.

52 Whitmore Road

Our next project in mass timber was 52 Whitmore Road, a mixed-use, seven-story building adjacent to Regent's Canal in London. I was one of four clients who together developed this brownfield site into a combination of affordable office space, double-height photographic studio, and three triple-height apartments. The finished building is timber inside and out. Clad in British sweet chestnut, it is at home behind a group of silver birch trees on its waterfront site.

Whitmore Road illustrates the structural capabilities of modern engineered timber and pushes the boundaries of timber design in new directions. At the center of the building is a vast double-height, column-free photo studio—an open space 30 feet deep and 75 feet long. Here the walls act as beams, and the party walls in the apartments above act as trusses. Nine- and twelve-inch-thick floor slabs allowed us to produce generous windows on the north facade along with the expansive studio.

The building maximizes the multilateral strength of CLT panels by minimizing lateral spans through careful arrangement of interior spaces. Structural fins, glulam beams, and custom fittings strengthen the north facade. These components help to transfer loads from a five-foot cantilever around the large window openings, down the front of the building, and back to the foundations.

Building in timber reduced the impact of 52 Whitmore Road on the environment from the conceptual design on. The structure includes 427 cubic meters of timber, which sequester approximately 106 tons of carbon—equivalent to 392 tons of carbon dioxide. Our analysis showed that an

52 WHITMORE ROAD
LONDON, ENGLAND
2012

Floor 4

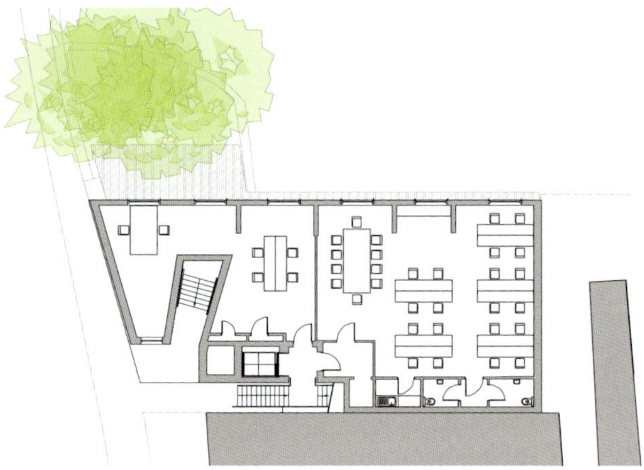

Floor 3

PLANS

Floor 1

SECTION

PANEL DIAGRAM

DAZED

equivalent structure with a concrete frame would have called for approximately 336 cubic meters of concrete, resulting in emissions of 105 tons of carbon dioxide. Therefore, by building in timber we prevented nearly 500 tons of carbon dioxide from entering the atmosphere.

A New Timber Architecture

The tectonic expression of mass timber is still developing. New technologies demand new forms. For centuries, material innovation has been a means with which to revitalize the traditions of architecture.

In our work with timber, two tasks have driven us forward. First, we have endeavored to prove to clients, contractors, and the authorities that code requirements can be met by timber just as they are met by concrete and steel. Second, we have attempted to pioneer a timber architecture with its own form of expression, perhaps even one that will inspire our contemporaries to take a step toward solid timber.

We continually challenge ourselves to deduce what is truly innovative about solid timber. Building in timber is quick, clean, and easy. It can be achieved with a measured accuracy and lack of noise, waste, or need for material storage. It has notable benefits in warmth, acoustics, and the structural feats possible. In a world ever more concentrated in urban areas, timber is the basis for safe and healthy cities composed of exceptionally designed and responsibly constructed buildings.

Andrew Waugh is a founding director of Waugh Thistleton Architects in London and a noted advocate for timber construction. In 2010 he was awarded the President's Medal of the Royal Institute for British Architects for his research into high-rise buildings in timber. Waugh lectures across the world with a focus on sustainability, timber construction, and the future of architecture and has taught at universities in England, Australia, Mexico, and the United States.

COMPETITION

INTRODUCTION

Innovation on the Waterfront

Andrew Bernheimer

To know New York City (to know any big city, truly) is to be familiar with the idea that a large metropolis consists of countless subcities and that each subcity faces its own challenges. A series of rather daunting tasks, then, is part of formulating a design competition that will challenge students and emerging professionals to reimagine (and even invent) new ways of building in these cities: identifying the "right" place for these visions to manifest themselves, devising the "right" building type to catalyze thinking around specific issues of urbanism, development, space-making, architecture, and technology. And all this without diluting the focus of the design challenge or distracting from the core principles of the competition.

For the Timber in the City competition, the right place is Red Hook, Brooklyn; the right building type is a mix of manufacturing and residential; and the core principle is to propose new structures built primarily of wood. The long tradition of timber building, the ingrained knowledge that most architects and architecture students have about the means and methods of this type of construction, is paradoxical. Most designers are utterly comfortable with the common stick-built structure, with the rapid, renewable, and cost-effective elements used to make innumerable American buildings. At the same time, despite being a proven way to build, wood construction is also something of a *modus non gratus* in modern cities. It is a building system for the suburbs, for the small city, but not for the metropolis. The New York City building code restricts the use of wood as a structural material. The tallest residential apartment building that may be constructed using combustible materials (such as timber) for exterior structure is three stories. It is obvious why this is the case. City authorities, city builders, and city dwellers alike fear fire and fragility. The systems of construction, as codified by building regulations, are shaped by a legacy of infernos that resulted from natural disaster and human error. The destruction of vast swaths of prominent cities, the real loss of life and property, and the memory of such disasters have embedded restrictions that, though seemingly sensible, have become obsolete.

Wood is no longer dangerous as a structural material for buildings higher than three stories—much higher. We have smartly codified systems for safety; we have the technology to satisfy these systems; and we now have the means to engineer and assemble natural, widely available, and renewable timber into systems that burn predictably and remain structurally robust. Yet such construction is still not allowed, at least not in New York City. This competition will, or should, prove to be the start of a reconsideration of these restrictions, and the entrants will, or should, inspire the hope that soon we will be able to execute new wood buildings in a dense city.

Although protection from fire was at issue throughout the conception of Timber in the City, the onslaught of Superstorm Sandy in October 2012, in the midst of the launch of the competition, prompted a renewed attention to other types of calamities. Sandy wreaked havoc on the East Coast and inundated the proposed site in Red Hook. Water rose to approximately fifteen feet above the mean water line and at this location on the harborfront was three to four feet above ground level. As a result, the competition brief was augmented to suggest that participants consider as additional context the preparation (or lack thereof) before the storm, the rise in water levels, and the recovery efforts initiated following the flood and investigate the possibilities offered by timber construction to foster resilience in the face of a changing urban and climatological environment. Although the site for the competition was in the most vulnerable part of the city, it remained viable due to existing public housing, the prevalence of industry and manufacturing, and the sheer value of empty land at the edge of the water. Sandy provided an opportunity to thrive rather than a reason to flee.

While manufacturing uses in New York and elsewhere have left the waterfront to make way for public parks and market-rate residential housing, Red Hook still maintains an active (though vastly changed) waterfront infrastructure. The neighborhood hosts New York City's outlet of Ikea, but also the Sixpoint Brewery and numerous other mid-scale manufacturers and even agricultural land. Red Hook also contains a mix of dense public housing and smaller single-family homes; nevertheless, the area is cut off from most city services (there is just one bus line running through the neighborhood, and no subways are close). Competitors were asked to propose a hub for affordable dwelling and urban manufacturing (both larger-scale production and smaller-scale making and learning), one that would address the specific assets and liabilities of the locality.

The competition program offered the opportunity to deploy multiple wood construction systems across multiple spatial conditions. Among the factors were cellularity of organization, potential modularity, spanning conditions, and surface materiality. Entrants were expected to investigate mass timber systems such as cross-laminated timber, panelized wood, and long-span members such as glulams and engineered trusses. But wood was not meant to be used only as structure, nor was it advised that competitors wrap their buildings in wood as a superficial nod to the theme. The program was formulated so that design visions would be driven by technology, so that spaces and forms would be composed by virtue of systemic adaptation or invention.

Over 1,000 participants—current students and recent graduates—submitted more than 200 entries to Timber in the City. Jurors Mark Cruvellier (Cornell University College of Architecture, Art, and Planning), Michael Green (MGA | Michael Green Architecture), Abby Hamlin (Hamlin Ventures), Alan Organschi (Gray Organschi Architecture, Yale School of Architecture), Tricia Stuth (University of Tennessee College of Architecture and Design), and Andrew Waugh (Waugh Thistleton Architects) congregated in New York and awarded honors to six entries. These premiated designs are galvanizing delineations of the future of design and construction. Although they are young, the winners are already at the leading edge of their chosen field, pursuing design concepts that will become commonplace. For that to happen, the optimism of those just entering the design professions must be matched by city governments, by builders, and by those of us who are practicing architects and educators.

FIRST

Grow Your Own City

Benjamin Bye
Alex Kenton
Jason Rood
University of Oregon

Faculty Sponsors
Judith Sheine, University of Oregon
Mikhail Gershfeld, Cal Poly Pomona

Grow Your Own City strives to celebrate, technically and aesthetically, cross-laminated timber building technology. Located in Red Hook, Brooklyn, the project is a hub for both assembly and deployment of Grow Your Own City CLT pods. Affordable living units, commercial spaces, and manufacturing facilities support a wide range of daily activities, inspire healthy community relations, and recognize the natural forests and ecosystem of the northeastern United States. The project epitomizes the Grow Your Own City process—plant, harvest, mill, transport, assemble, stack, live—and motto—"Plant a tree, grow a city."

Grow Your Own City builds on the rich natural and cultural history of Red Hook. The live/work pods wrap the site and are disposed to maximize access to light, air, and views. Modular units ranging from studios to three bedrooms are stacked into low-rise and tower housing. At ground level, a bicycle shop, restaurant, digital fabrication labs, and green alley highlight the culture and community of Red Hook.

The green alley, an urban park on the interior of the site, supports recreational activities, community functions, and festivals. Designed as an educational walk, the alley showcases the lumber industry and the production of cross-laminated timber and other mass timber products. The green space also demonstrates sustainable practices: rainwater harvesting, solar energy collection, and habitat rehabilitation and ecosystem recovery.

Grow Your Own City CLT pods can be assembled, finished, and shipped from the site. The modular building concept takes advantage of the material properties, strength, and dimensions of cross-laminated timber. CLT panels act as both load-bearing and shear walls in high- and low-rise buildings. The exposed walls consist of solid CLT and floor-to-ceiling windows. The outer faces of the different pod types form a pattern on the facades of the structures, generating regularity and variety. The standardization of pods (one 325-square-foot pod for a studio, two pods for a one-bedroom unit, two and a half pods for a two-bedroom unit, and three pods for a three-bedroom unit) and low embodied cost of CLT contribute to affordability and environmental friendliness. The digital fabrication lab allows for the customization of pod dimensions and types.

The Grow Your Own City pod offers the potential to extend beyond the Red Hook site. Prefabricated, stackable, and transportable, the pods can be transplanted and grown anywhere. Once the initial Grow Your Own City buildings are completed, the on-site manufacturing plant will continue to drive the economy of Red Hook.

CONSTRUCTION TIMELINE

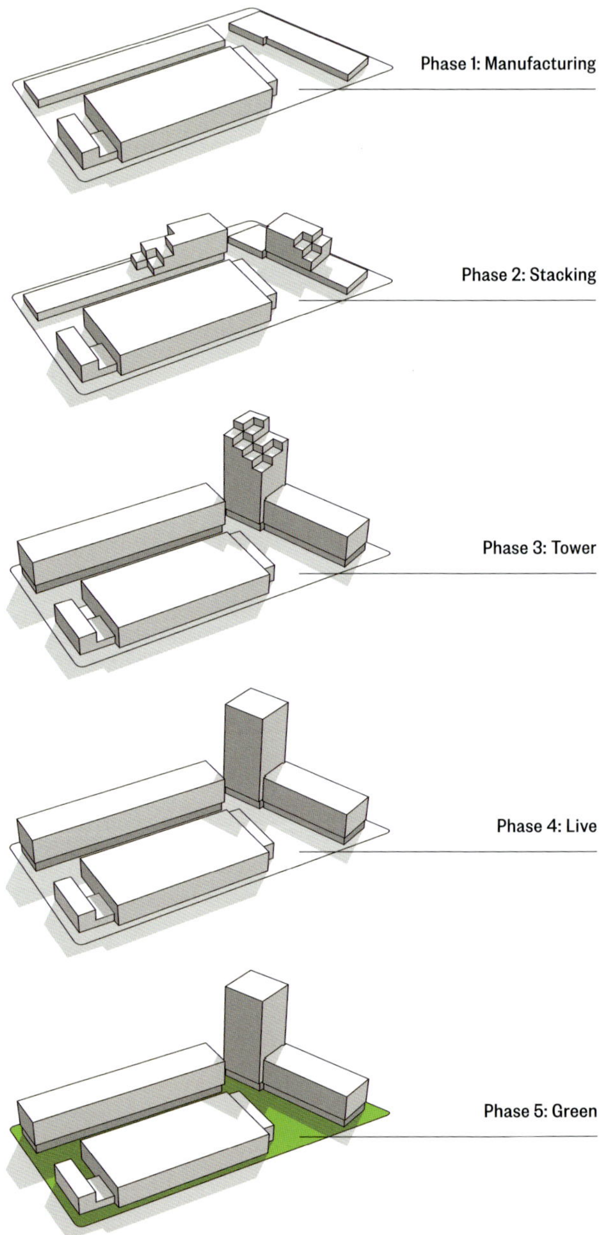

Brewery
Café
Pub
Light industry
Grow Your Own City
Community farm
CLT panels delivered to port
Erie Basin Park
Ikea

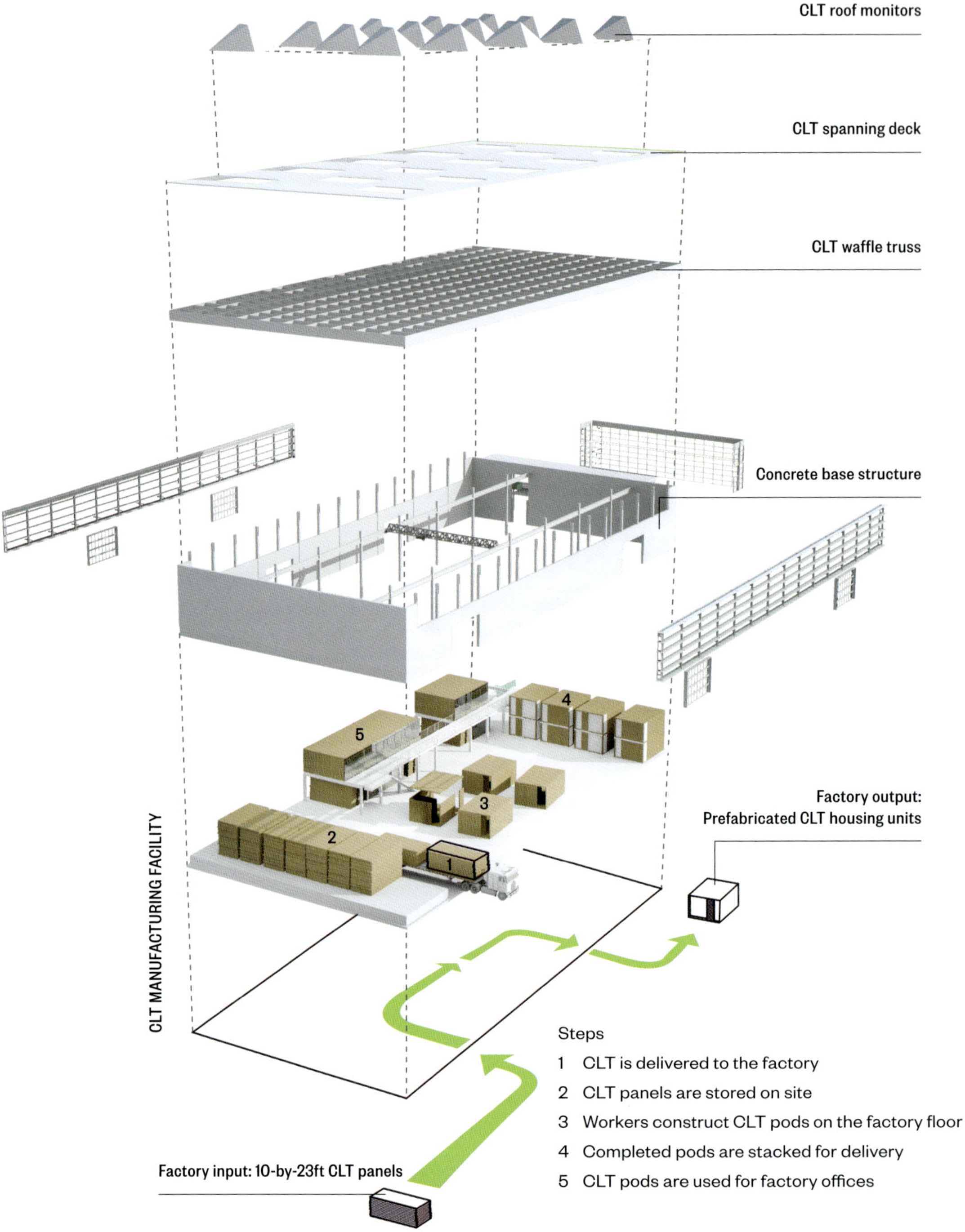
CLT roof monitors
CLT spanning deck
CLT waffle truss
Concrete base structure
CLT MANUFACTURING FACILITY
Factory output:
Prefabricated CLT housing units
Factory input: 10-by-23ft CLT panels
1
2
3
4
5
Steps
1 CLT is delivered to the factory
2 CLT panels are stored on site
3 Workers construct CLT pods on the factory floor
4 Completed pods are stacked for delivery
5 CLT pods are used for factory offices

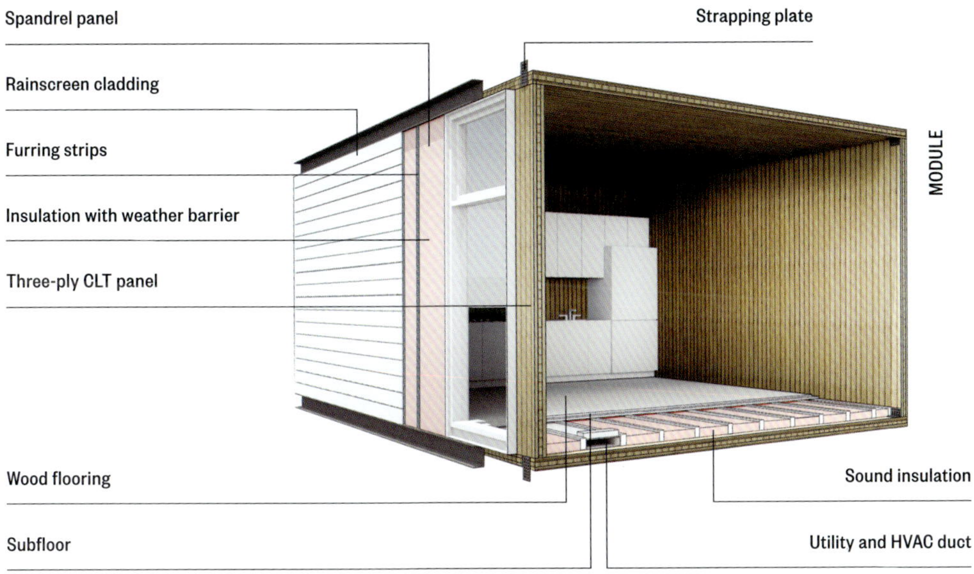
Spandrel panel
Strapping plate
Rainscreen cladding
Furring strips
Insulation with weather barrier
Three-ply CLT panel
MODULE
Wood flooring
Sound insulation
Subfloor
Utility and HVAC duct

Studio
1 pod
105 units
330 sq ft

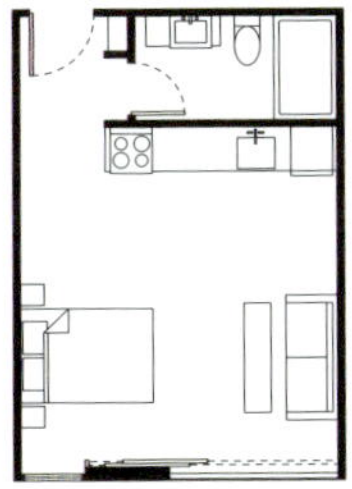

One Bedroom
2 pods
45 units
660 sq ft

Two Bedrooms
2.5 pods
32 units
825 sq ft

Three Bedrooms
3 pods
18 units
990 sq ft

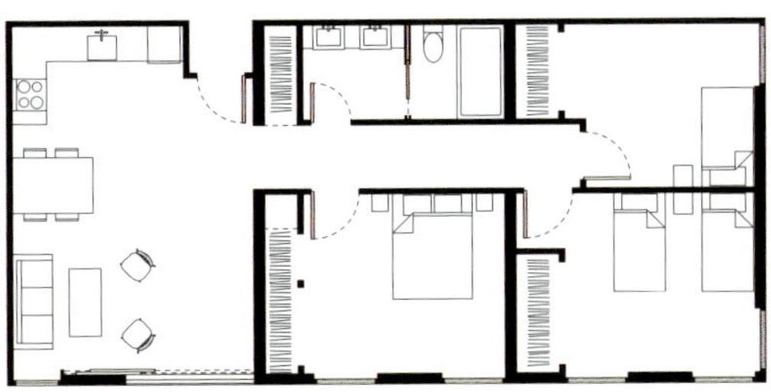

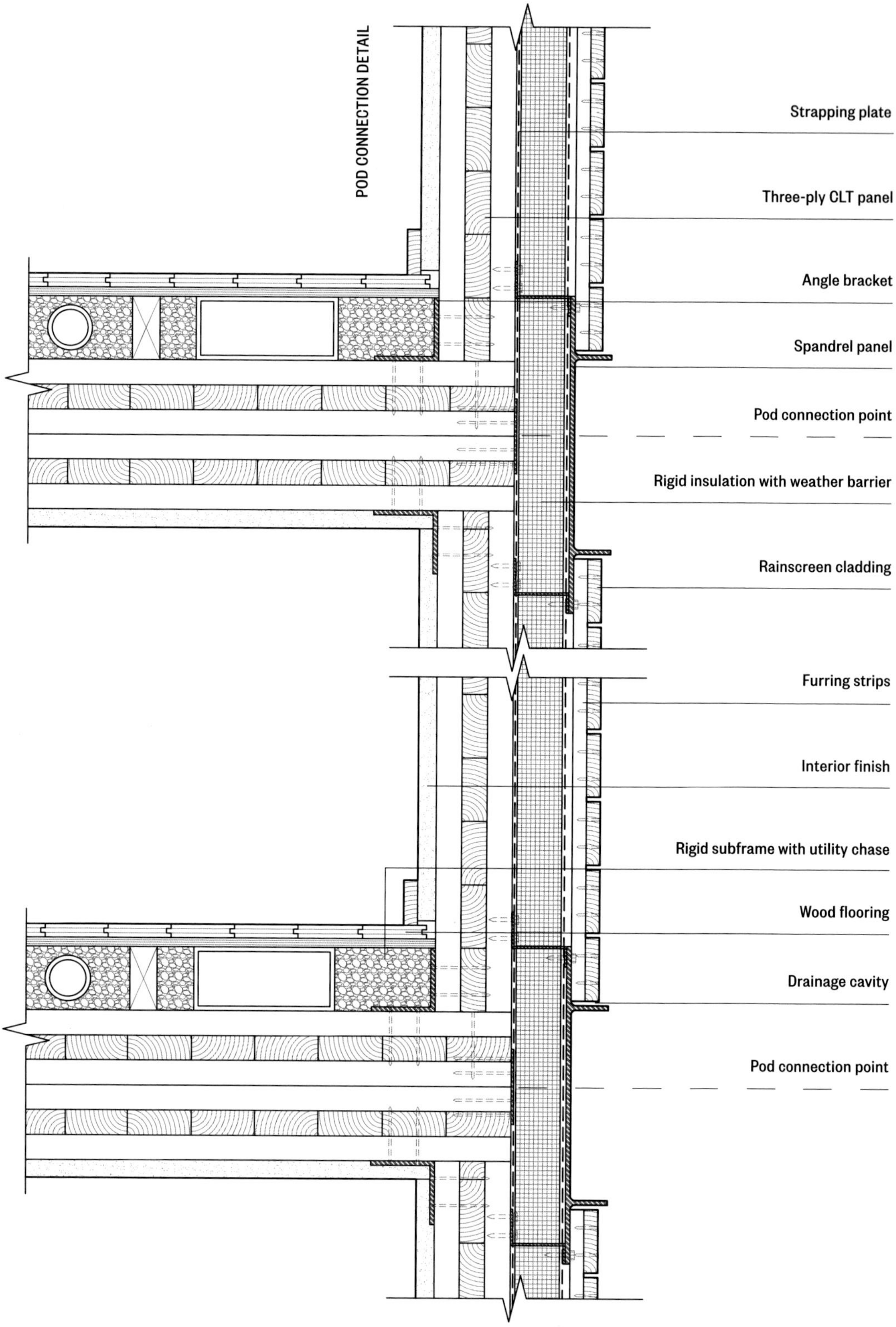
POD CONNECTION DETAIL
Strapping plate
Three-ply CLT panel
Angle bracket
Spandrel panel
Pod connection point
Rigid insulation with weather barrier
Rainscreen cladding
Furring strips
Interior finish
Rigid subframe with utility chase
Wood flooring
Drainage cavity
Pod connection point

KAVANAGH
KAVANAGH CRANE HIRE LTD

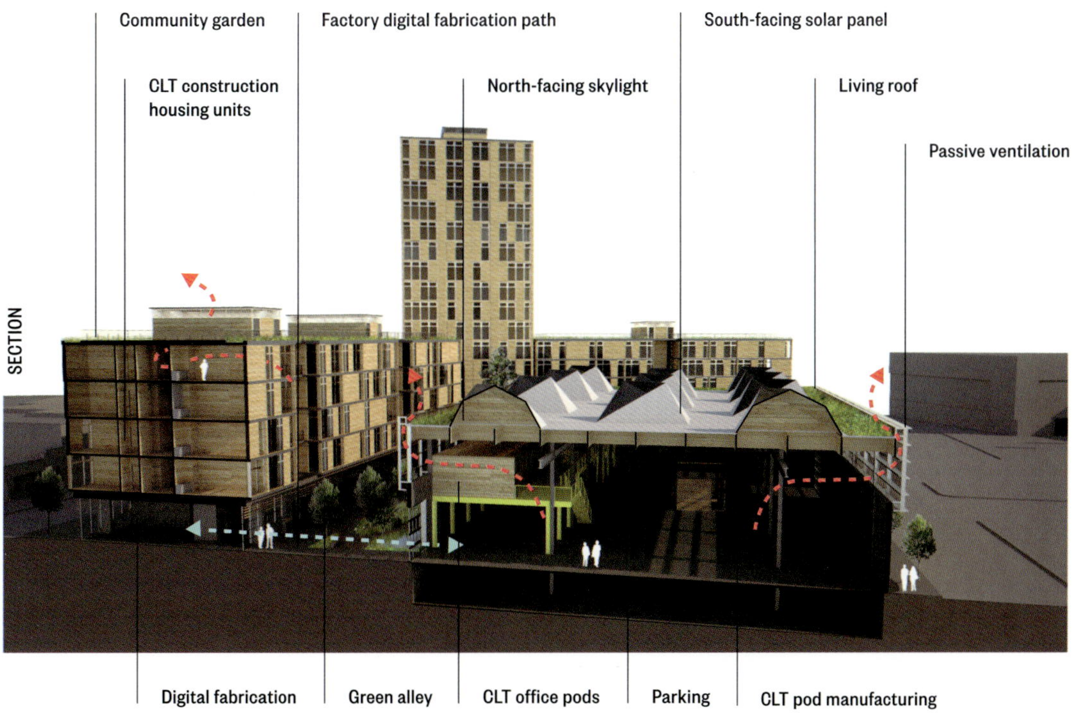
SECTION
Community garden
Factory digital fabrication path
South-facing solar panel
CLT construction housing units
North-facing skylight
Living roof
Passive ventilation
Digital fabrication
Green alley
CLT office pods
Parking
CLT pod manufacturing

SECOND

Cultivating Timber

Christopher Gardner
University of Texas at Austin

Faculty Sponsor
Ulrich Dangel, University of Texas at Austin

Timber has yet to enter the mainstream of building technology in the United States despite its clear advantages. More sustainable and more efficient than typical construction materials, timber has the potential to change the way buildings are built. Cultivating Timber plants the seeds for this change in Red Hook.

The project incorporates timber manufacturing and distribution, public education, and low-income housing. These disparate functions revolve around an on-site factory for the production of timber products. The production facility, established as the first component on the site, manufactures the rest of the development. Currently, the means of production for CLT exists primarily in Canada, Europe, and New Zealand. But a supply of softwood lumber is readily available in the Northeast. Barge shipments of lumber to the site allow production with local materials, revitalize a historic artery of New York, and drastically reduce greenhouse gases and embodied energy.

Cultivating Timber progresses in stages, embracing its own construction. Phase one includes the renovation of an existing building as a hiring facility and showroom. Foundations, the only use of concrete on the site, are poured in phase two. The third phase introduces production machinery and local lumber. Temporary canopies shelter production while the framing for the factory is manufactured. In phase four, the machinery is installed in the newly assembled factory and production commences on the rest of the site. The tower rises quickly in phase five. The sixth phase consists of the completion and inhabitation of the tower. The site is fully activated as the factory begins the manufacture of timber products for use outside the site.

The ground floor is devoted to public programs, with parking located below grade. Digital and wood production facilities on the second floor are protected from potential flood damage. The open plan of the factory is easily adapted to future timber technology. An on-site cogeneration plant utilizes off-cuts from the factory to power the site.

The centerpiece of the ground level is a public lawn that slopes up to allow views into the factory; sheltered beneath is a large bike storage facility. The surrounding commercial areas encourage local businesses to reinvest in Red Hook, connecting the site to the community. The tower, comprising 175 residential units and constructed entirely out of CLT, demonstrates the most innovative use of timber on the site. The shear walls at the center provide rigidity and centralize services; the perpendicular party walls stabilize the building laterally. These party walls allow variation in unit placement.

Phase 3

Phase 4

Phase 5

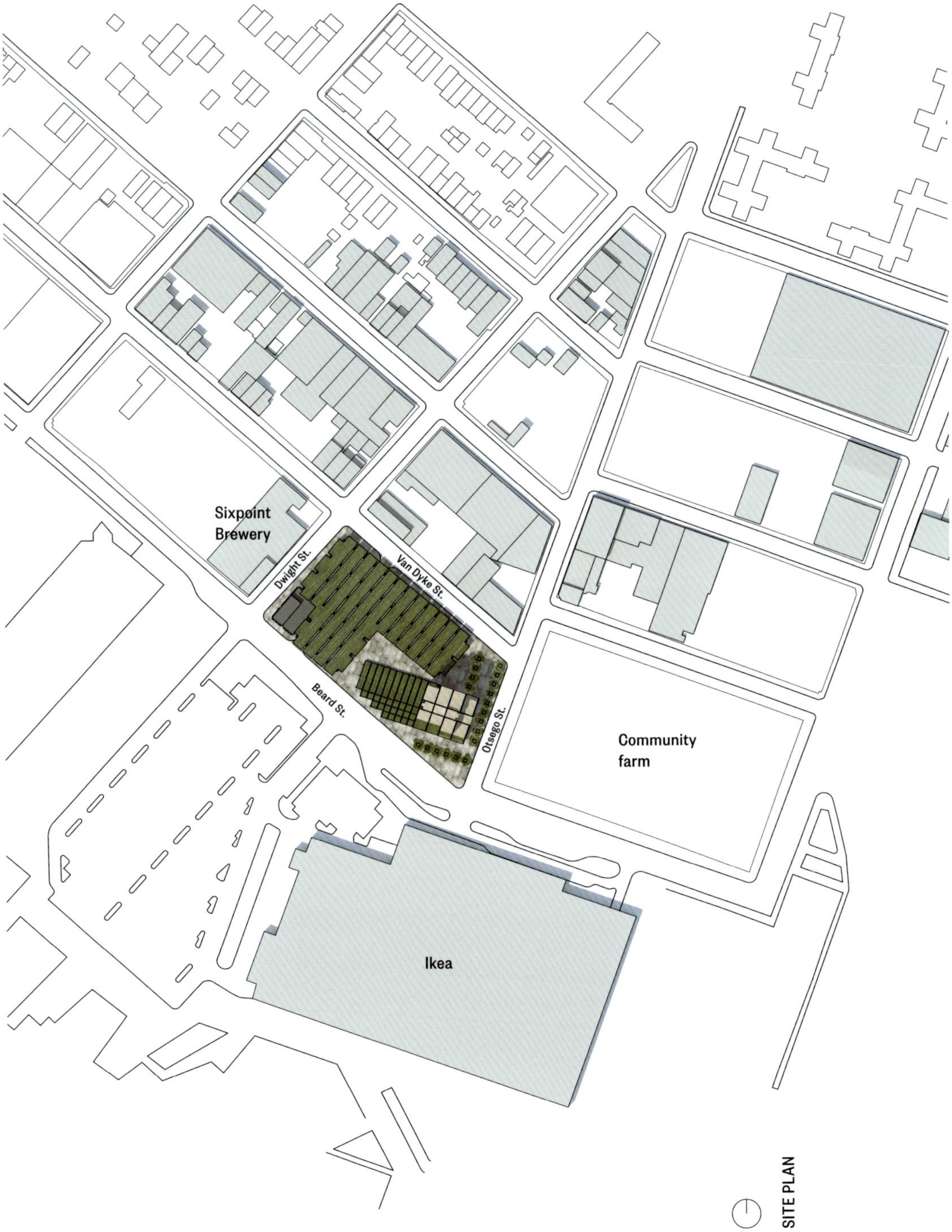
Sixpoint
Brewery
Dwight St.
Van Dyke St.
Beard St.
Otsego St.
Community
farm
Ikea

SITE PLAN

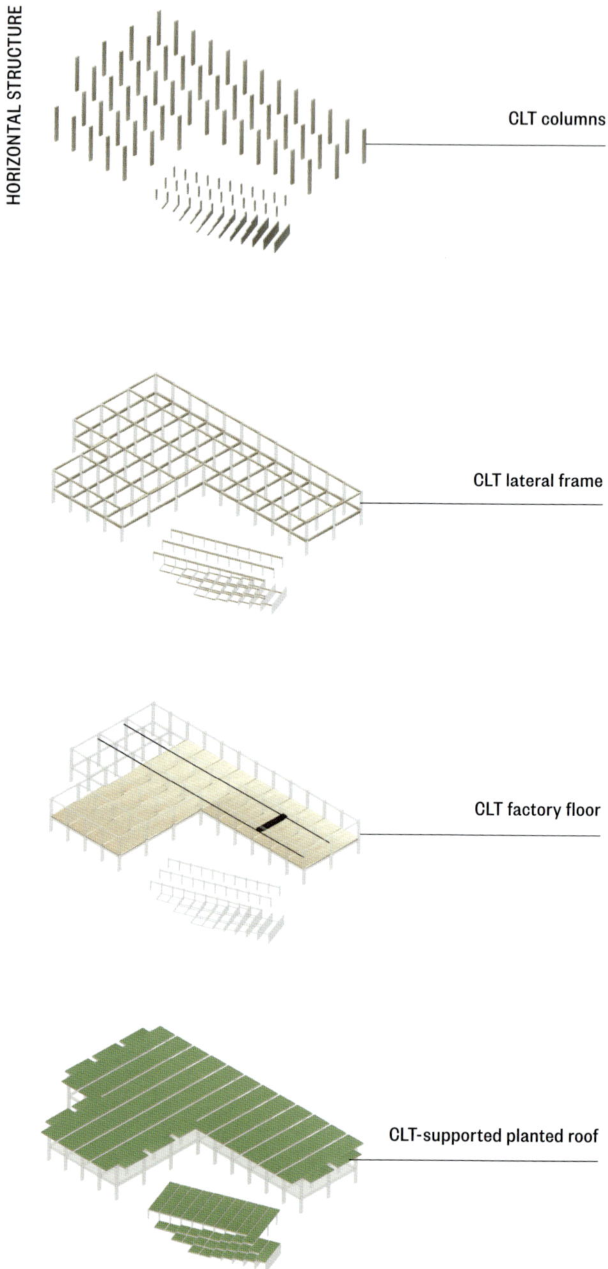
HORIZONTAL STRUCTURE
CLT columns
CLT lateral frame
CLT factory floor
CLT-supported planted roof

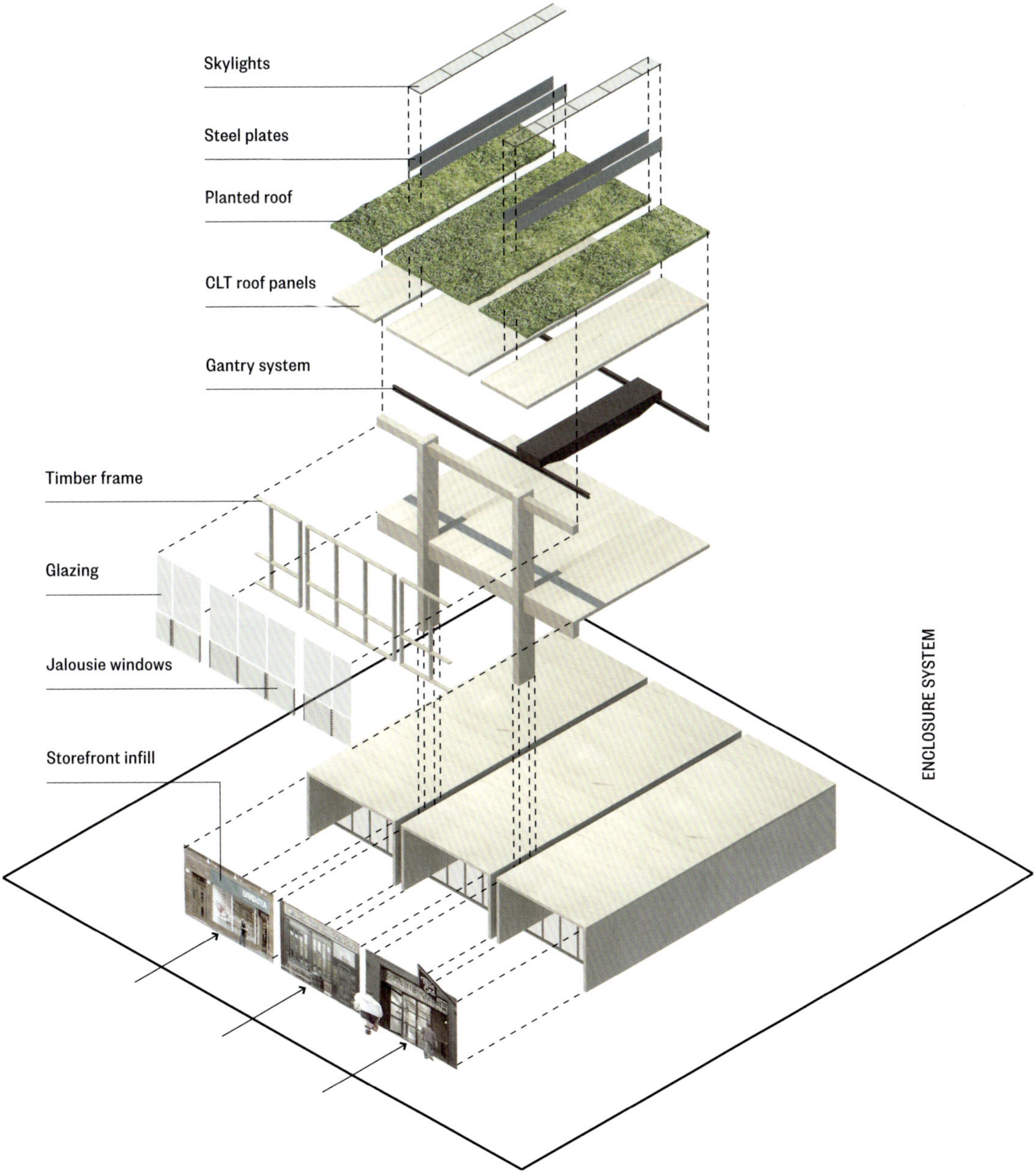
Skylights
Steel plates
Planted roof
CLT roof panels
Gantry system
Timber frame
Glazing
Jalousie windows
Storefront infill

PLANS

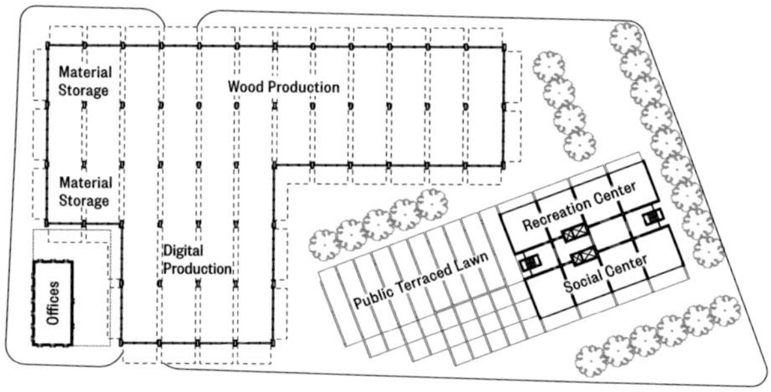

Floor 2

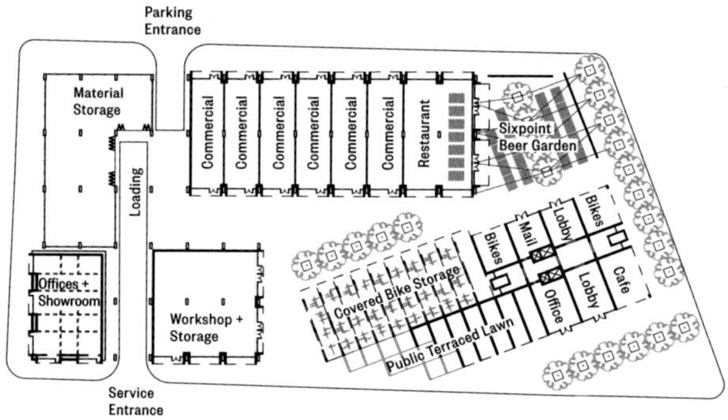

Floor 1

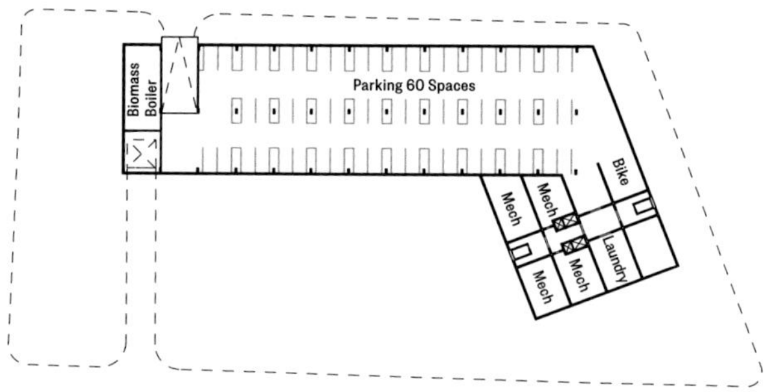

Underground floor

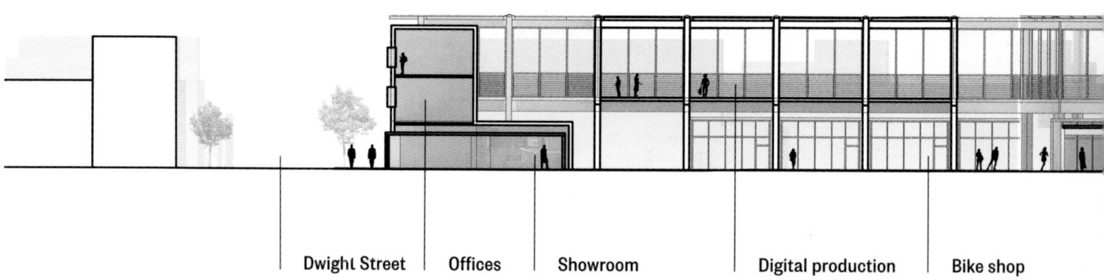

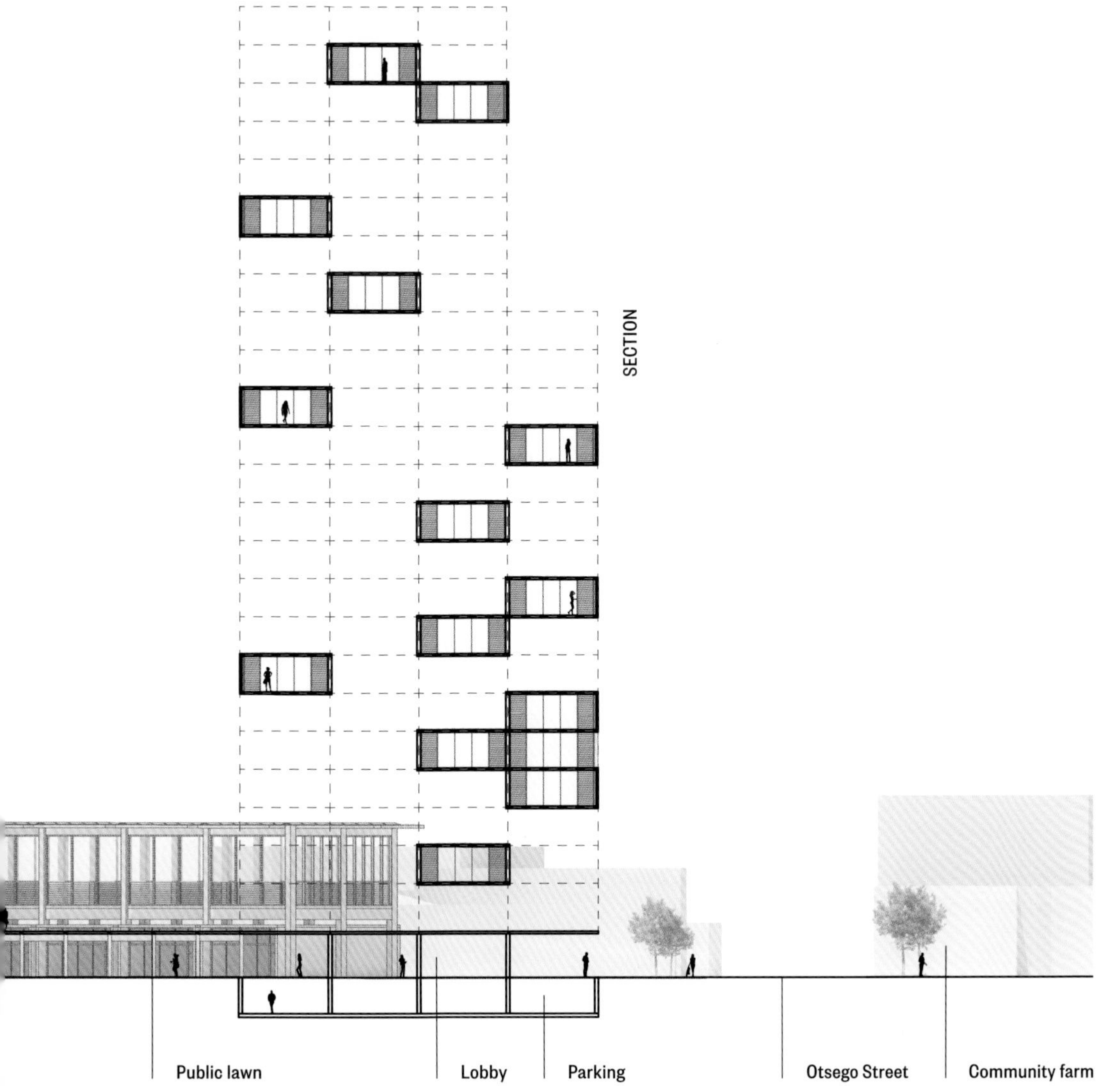

SECTION

Swamp Machine

MENTION

Benjamin Ahearn
Kristin Karlsson
Carey Moran
University of Washington

Faculty Sponsors
Richard Mohler and Elizabeth Golden, University of Washington

Manifesting as a series of planned events, the Swamp Machine is both enterprise and architecture, or enterprise as architecture. Creating a habitat for industry, for inhabitation, for recreation, for bioremediation, the Swamp Machine enhances the coastline of Red Hook by reinstating native ecology. The swamp returns to Red Hook, and Red Hook returns to the swamp.

The first step in the transformation is a digital fabrication workshop, which slips into a brick building on the corner of Beard and Dwight Streets. The fences surrounding the property vanish; the ground begins to drop. The landscape changes, not only with the seasons but with the weather. Boardwalks layered over the wetlands make the site accessible to the community. Residents carve new paths and shortcuts. Industry and commerce arrive: a bike shop, a wood shop and showcase of Swamp Machine fabrication capabilities, local outreach. Occupation is the final stage: housing fins enunciate the careful balance that constitutes the Swamp Machine.

The varied functions of the project populate a composite timber structure. The innovative construction system bespeaks its own potential, seeding and propagating timber technology. The cladding stops short of the ground, leaving the sparse structure as the only point of contact and creating a perceptible link between the site and the swamp. The Swamp Machine gathers material and labor resources from the region, creating opportunity in Red Hook. Yet the merging of intent and function spreads beyond the site, beyond Brooklyn.

The wood shop, digital workshop, bike shop, and housing, together with the landscape, create the machine. The wood shop, at the heart of the site, is the most vibrant and visible constituent. The engineered timber housing developed within appears initially in the housing fins on the site. The pavilion for the bike shop reveals the construction and design capabilities of the digital workshop and the wood shop together. The housing is linked to the landscape and the workshop. Lifted on plinths, the fins are islands in the wetlands. A symbiotic relationship occurs where the residential overlaps with the industrial. Structural hierarchies are blurred, mechanical services are shared, and visual connections are established.

The Swamp Machine begins as a vision. The plans are laid out, the wheels turn, the machine slowly engages. The land is manipulated, carved back to the water. Industry, commerce, and population follow and augment. Working within its environment the Swamp Machine expands an economy, enriches a community, renews a habitat. Each piece is essential; each contributes to a systematic symbiosis in Red Hook. Give it back, back to Brooklyn, back to the Swamp.

STEP 1

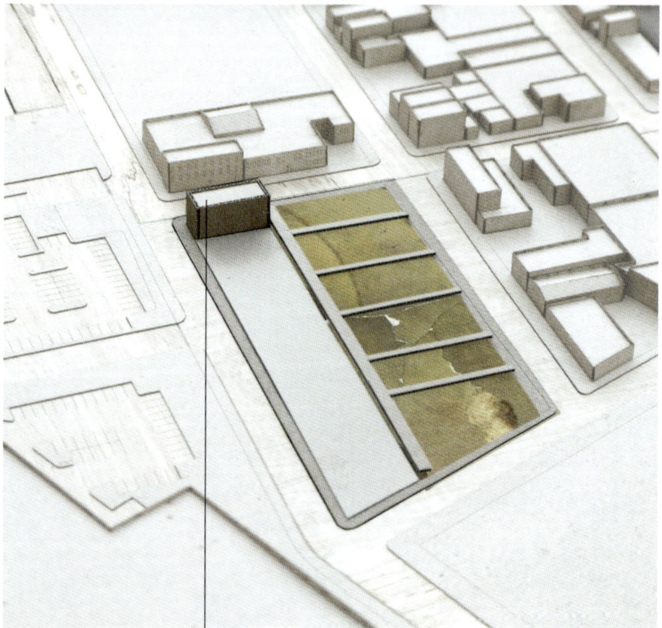

Digital fabrication workshop

THE BUILDING, BUILDING ITSELF

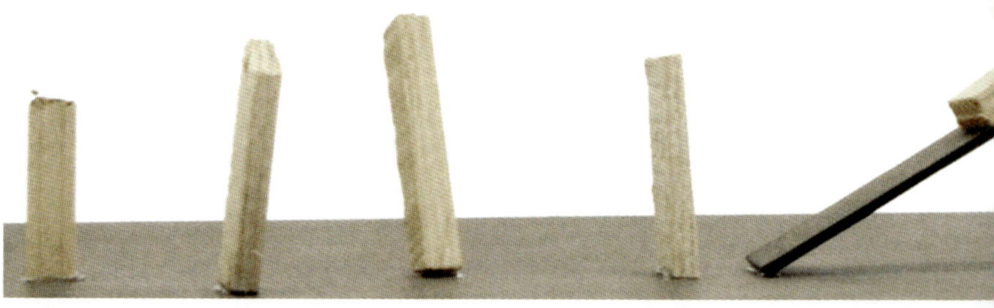

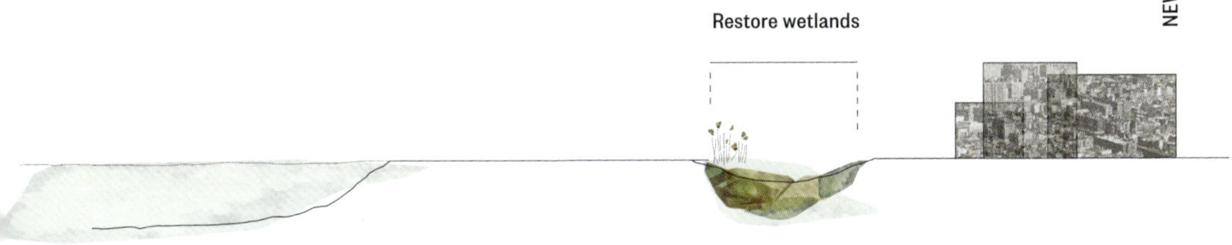
Restore wetlands

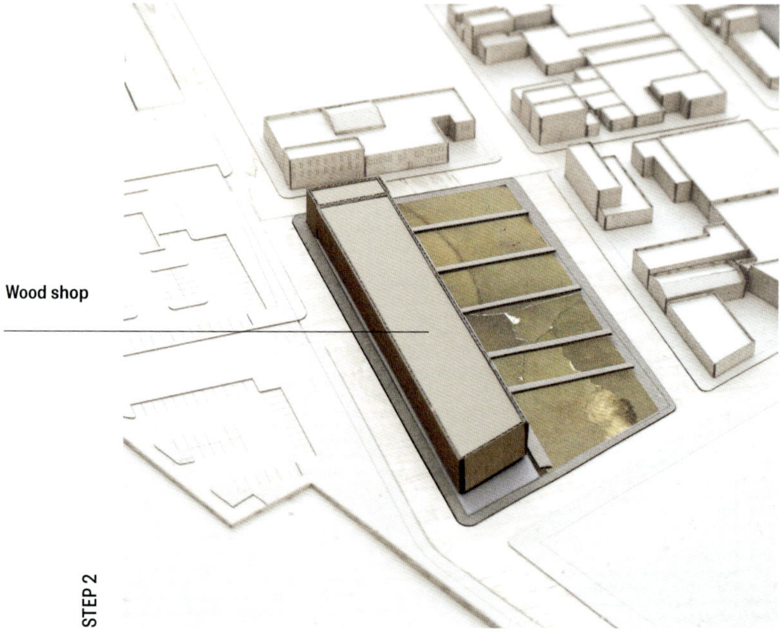

STEP 2

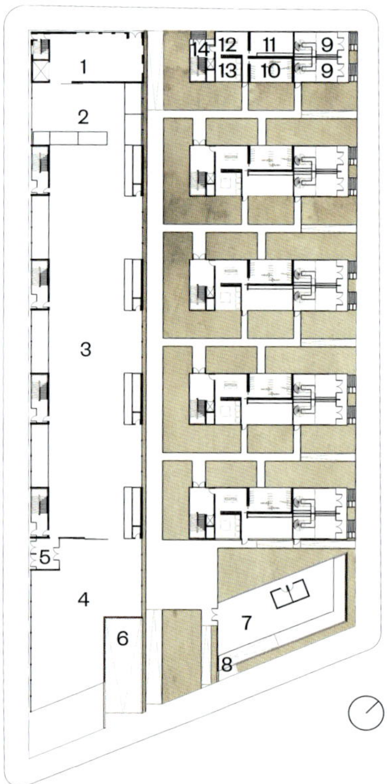

PLAN

1 Digital fabrication
2 Wood shop loading
3 Main production
4 Finish/assembly
5 Main entry, wood shop
6 Underground parking entrance
7 Bike shop
8 Ramp to maintenance
9 Storefront
10 Bike parking
11 Recreation room
12 Mailroom
13 Laundry
14 Main entry, housing

1 CLT
2 Vertical tongue-and-groove siding panel fabricated by the wood shop
3 Window
4 Fascia panel
5 Hybrid steel and wood truss
6 Steel connection fabricated by the digital workshop
7 Glulam beam

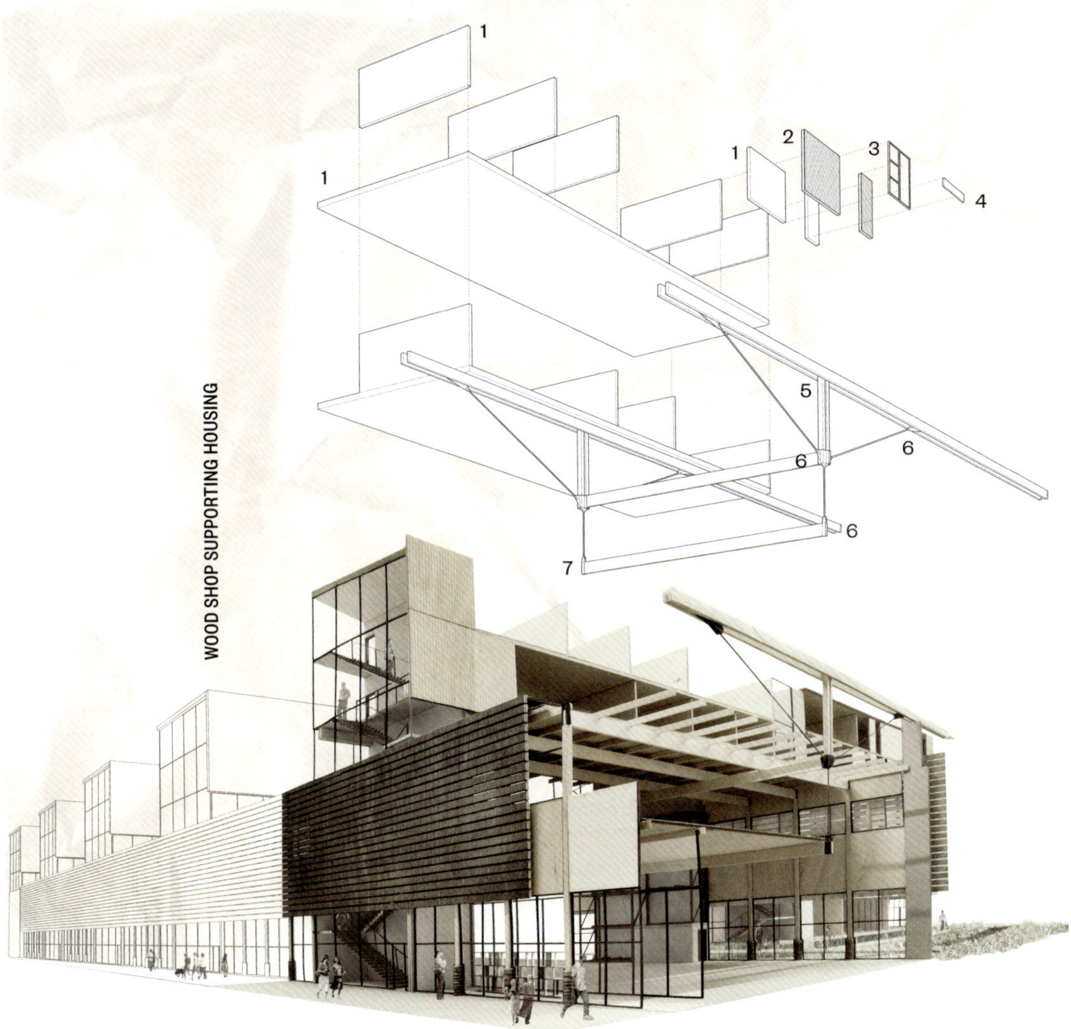

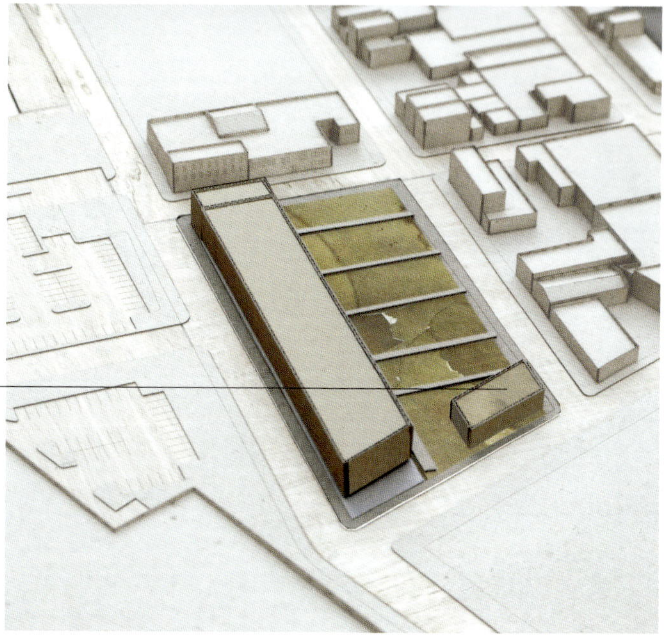

STEP 3

1 CLT
2 Glulam beam
3 King post truss
4 Wood column
5 Concrete core
6 Concrete plinth

STRUCTURE

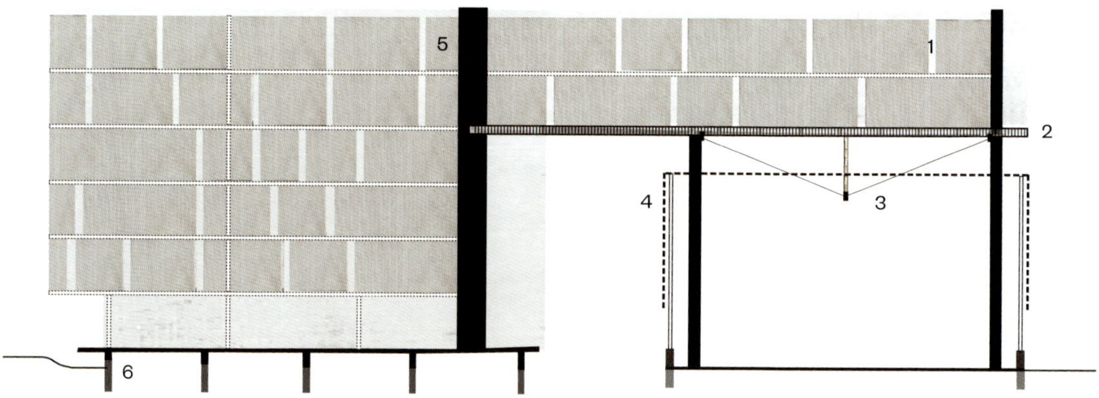

STEP 4

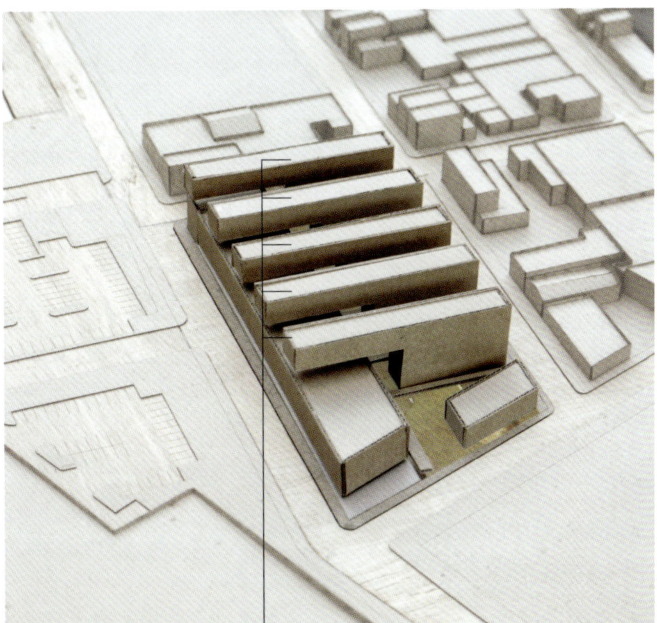

Housing

IKEA
IKEA
Please remain seated or hold rails while Water Taxi is in motion.

MENTION

House of Wood

Emily Hagen
Virginia Tech

Faculty Sponsor
Heinrich Schnoedt, Virginia Tech

The form of the project oscillates between House and Ware-House, asserting a representational difference between working and living. The traditional configurations of House and Ware-House are appropriated and then combined to create a hybrid typology that accommodates residential, commercial, and industrial uses.

The outer facade is a weave of wooden cladding that during the day makes the structures into a singular object. At night, interior light pierces the weave, revealing the complex activity level of a typical urban structure. The cladding is disposed to differentiate the two parts of the project visually; yet at the same time it enhances spatial performance. On the House, the weave is horizontal, allowing natural light to penetrate into the apartment spaces; on the Ware-House, the weave is vertical, admitting into the workspace only indirect light. On the ground floor of the Ware-House, bicycles may be parked between the vertical members. The primary structural element in both structures is the glulam column. Single columns divide the spaces in the Ware-House while doubled columns embrace the walls between apartment units in the House. The columns are aligned with the linearity of each building's form, dividing and orienting users throughout the building and allowing for geometric rationalization of the interior spaces.

The geometries of the New York City street grid regulate the forms of House and Ware-House and are carried through the site by means of the structural columns. The Ware-House makes reference to the Red Hook Community Farm across the street; the House instead cuts through the site, and through the Ware-House, to emphasize the linearity of the residential neighborhoods to the west. The junction between the two grids is a central gallery space that displays work built in the Ware-House to the community living in and around the House. The meeting of the two programs and the two forms produces a microcommunity within the larger city context.

SITE GRID

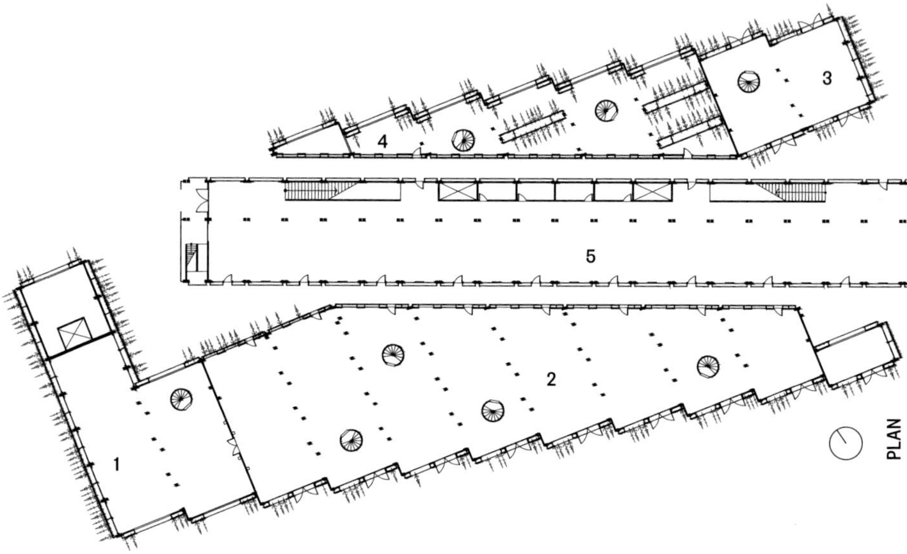

1 Wood storage

2 Pop-up shop

3 Bike shop/storage

4 Protected bike storage

5 Galleria/exhibition halls

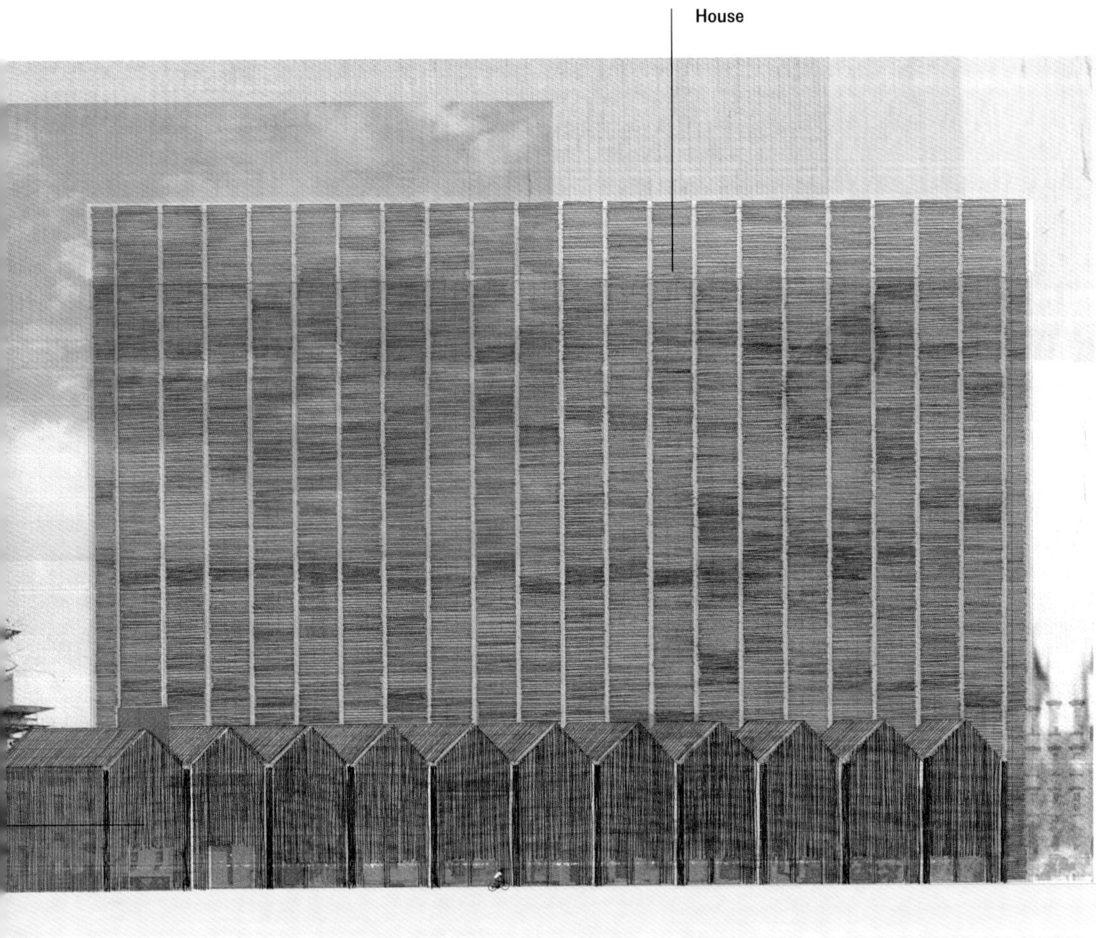
House

BICYCLE PARKING FACADE

SECTION

BICYCLE SHOP
THE HABITAT

MENTION

The Habitat @ Red Hook

Samuel Pitnick
B.Arch., 2010
University of Southern California

Set along the waterfront of Brooklyn's Red Hook neighborhood, the Habitat is a mixed-use complex that activates the surrounding community and reinvigorates local manufacturing and housing. The primary construction material and technology—mass timber—helped to drive the concept and design of the project. Heavy timber columns and beams are accentuated throughout. Operable wood screens along the south facades of the building highlight the dynamic qualities of wood. These elements educate visitors and residents alike about innovative wood construction.

The design and massing of the Habitat are generated by context and program. The overall square footage is split into two "bars," four- and six-story components that contain 175 residential units over ground-floor commercial space and wood and digital fabrication shops. The workshops are combined into a single entity, maximizing efficiency. Job training, education, and manufacturing are located along Van Dyke Street. Bicycle parking, storage, and workshops are placed along Beard Street. An elevated public walkway, reminiscent of the High Line park, and resident gardens are located between the bars. At the east end of the site, the building mass is pulled away to create a public plaza and establish the primary entrance. The lower, south building permits more natural light to penetrate the center of the site and the units in the north bar.

The studio and one-, two-, and three-bedroom affordable living units at the Habitat are constructed on a module of 12.5 by 25 feet. The units are assembled in the wood and digital fabrication shops on the ground floor, saving time and money, reducing construction waste, and cutting down on carbon emissions. The walls are formed of structural insulated panels, which offer thermal and acoustic insulation. Residents can customize kitchen and bathroom areas. Most units also feature balconies.

Glulam beams form a wood pedestal above the ground floor that supports the load of the units, which are hoisted into place by a crane. Stair and elevator cores are fabricated from cross-laminated timber panels, reducing the weight of the structure. The south facades of the Habitat are fashioned from recycled wood pallets. Forming a building face that can be manipulated by the residents, the pallet composition provides varying degrees of shade and privacy throughout the day.

In 2012, Hurricane Sandy brought massive flooding and property damage to Red Hook. Concrete construction within the flood plain and wood construction above safeguard against future damage. The operable wood facades, which can be fully closed, are a further precaution.

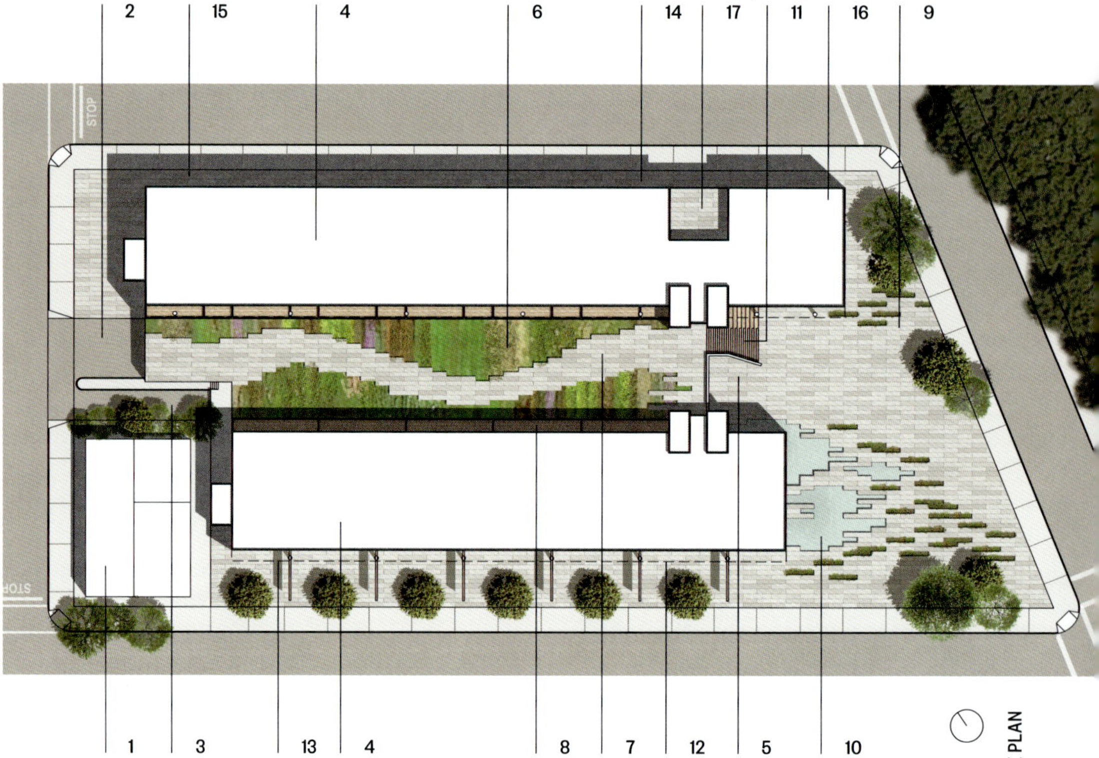

SITE PLAN

1 Existing building
2 Entrance to parking
3 Loading dock
4 Residential units
5 Entrance to resident lobby
6 Resident gardens
7 Public walkway
8 Resident patios
9 Public plaza and gardens
10 Water feature
11 Amphitheater seating and steps
12 Entrance to bike parking and shop
13 Bike workshop and maintenance
14 Digital/wood workshop and classrooms
15 Digital/wood showroom
16 Resident recreation area
17 Private resident terrace

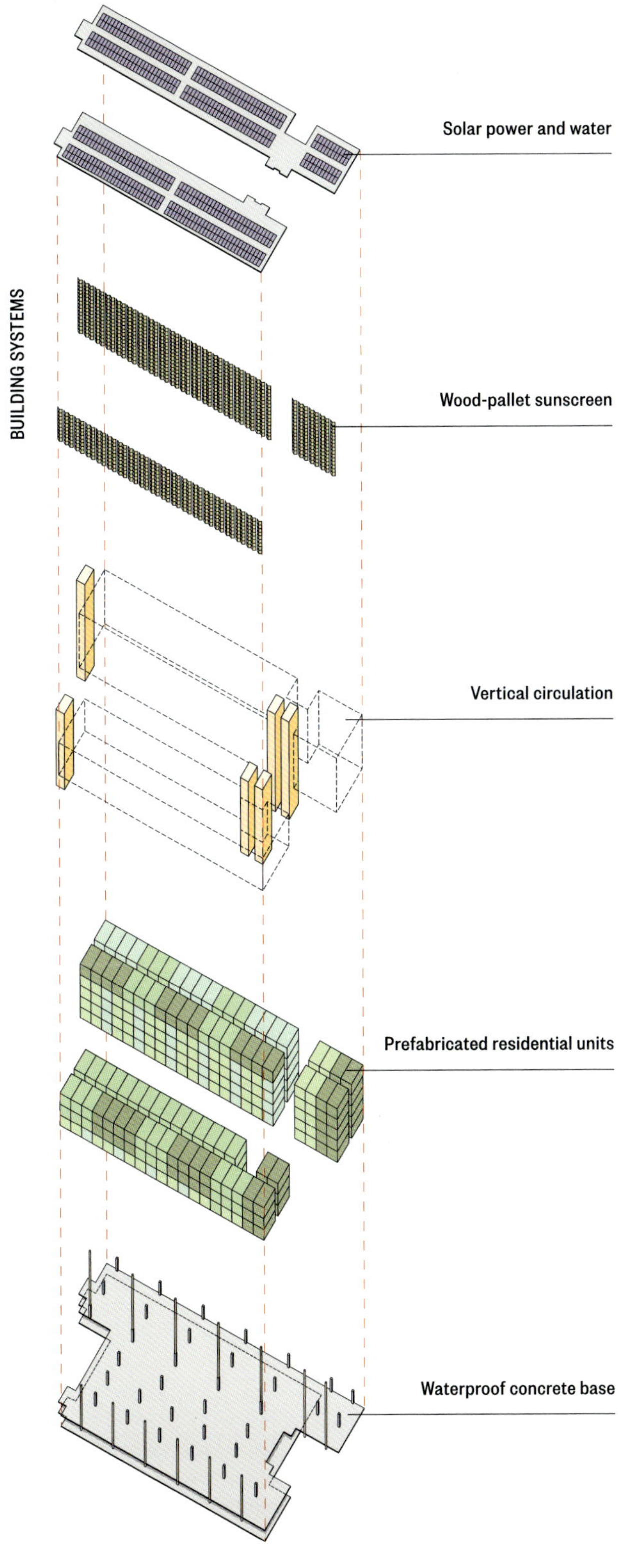
BUILDING SYSTEMS
Solar power and water
Wood-pallet sunscreen
Vertical circulation
Prefabricated residential units
Waterproof concrete base

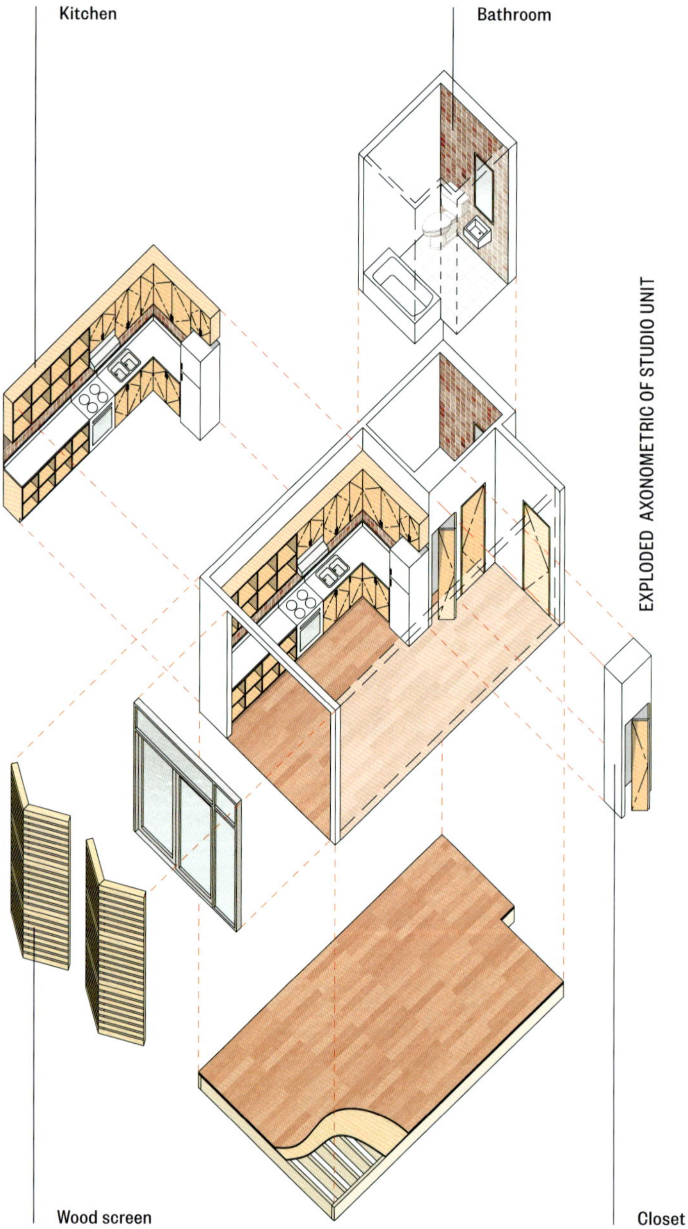

EXPLODED AXONOMETRIC OF STUDIO UNIT

PLANS

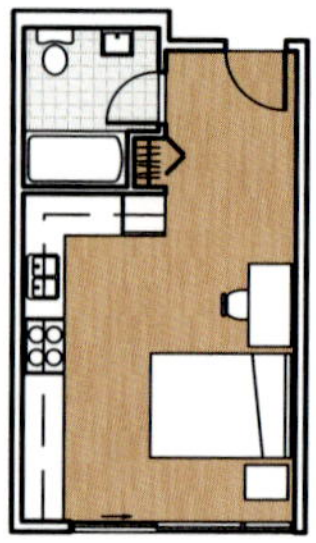

Studio
325 sq ft

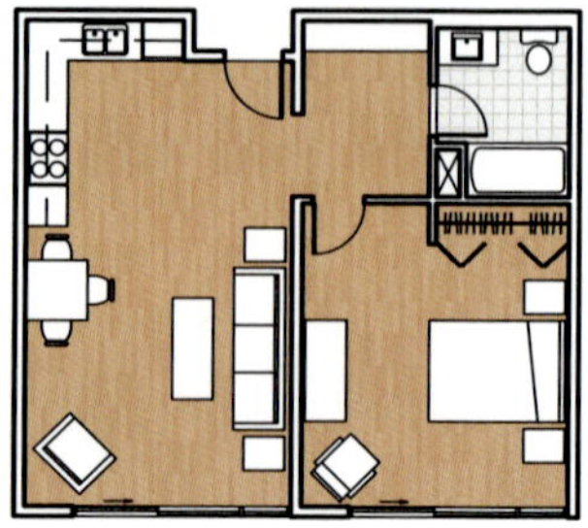

One Bedroom
650 sq ft

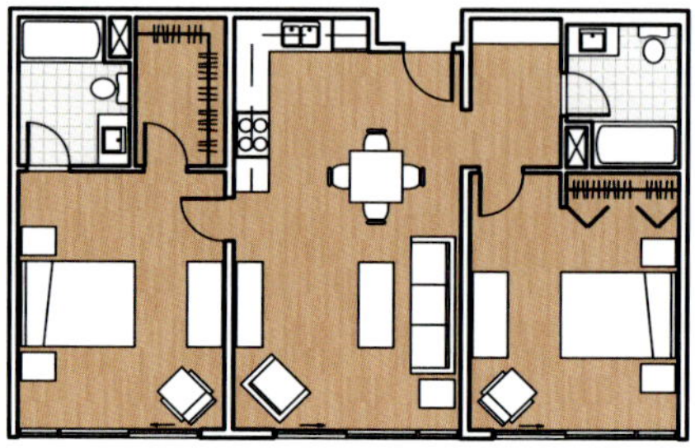

Two Bedrooms
850 sq ft

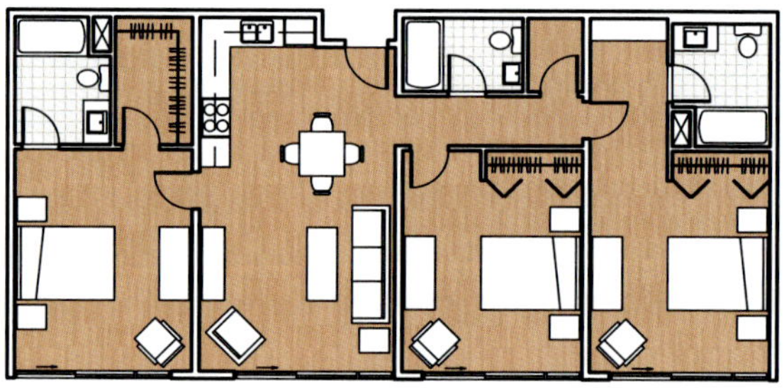

Three Bedrooms A
1,000 sq ft

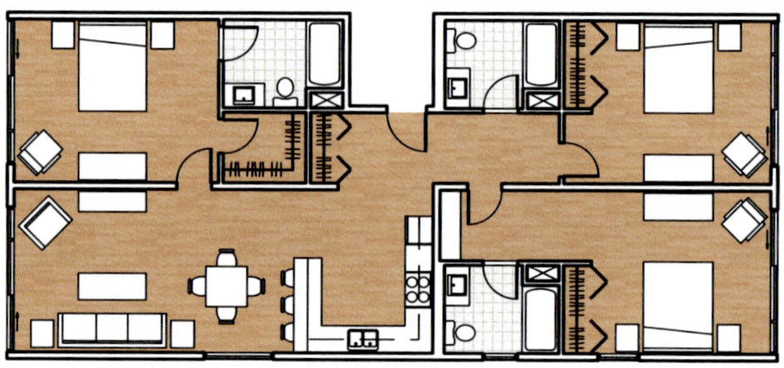

Three Bedrooms B
1,000 sq ft

THE HABITAT
@RED HOOK
◀DIGITAL SHOP
◀WOOD SHOP
◀CLASSROOMS
◀SHOWROOM

MENTION

Courtyard Cathedral

Timothy Olson
M.Arch., 2012
Massachusetts Institute of Technology

The Courtyard Cathedral leverages two complementary structural systems in mass timber to organize program, establish urban strategy, and influence architectural expression. The first is cross-laminated timber. CLT walls and shear and floor panels are the basis of three ten-story perimeter blocks accommodating apartments, offices, and retail. Within each of the blocks is a courtyard; large-scale voids notched into the apartment structure provide access and light to the courtyard spaces and create elevated, covered exterior decks for the residences on the upper floors. The 22-foot structural grid of the CLT facilitates a modular apartment strategy that anticipates changing market conditions in Brooklyn. A single bay furnishes a 350-square-foot apartment as well as a circulation pathway. Larger apartment units are created by combining bays.

The secondary structural system consists of interlocking two-way glulam roof vaults, braced by the perimeter blocks, that span the courtyard spaces. These vaults shelter bike share, wood shop, and digital fabrication facilities. The vaulting provides the long, uninterrupted spans required by the large scale and demand for flexibility of the interior functions. Hoods extending from the vaulted roofs project through the voids in the CLT perimeter at the first floor. These extensions of the courtyard roofs provide a public face and entry point for the establishments within as well as covered public space and protected outdoor bike storage. A three-foot gap between the courtyard and the apartment perimeter facilitates drainage and creates a service chase for mechanical equipment. The gap also accommodates circulation and storage and mitigates sound transmission.

The perimeter blocks are clad in a double-skin facade. A single pane of glass is a weatherproof membrane that protects the wooden structure within. Structural insulated panels and insulated glazing units are located inside the glass and create a thermal division between inside and out.

The location on Van Dyke Street promotes denser commercial and pedestrian activity along this corridor. Divisions between the buildings create pathways that connect the project to the waterfront to the south. A service corridor parallels Van Dyke Street, and parking is situated below. An earthen stormbreak on the south side of the site creates an elevated park that augments the green spaces of adjacent parcels.

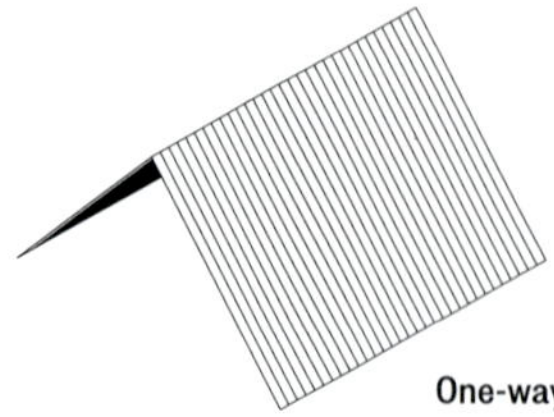

One-way vault

SECTION

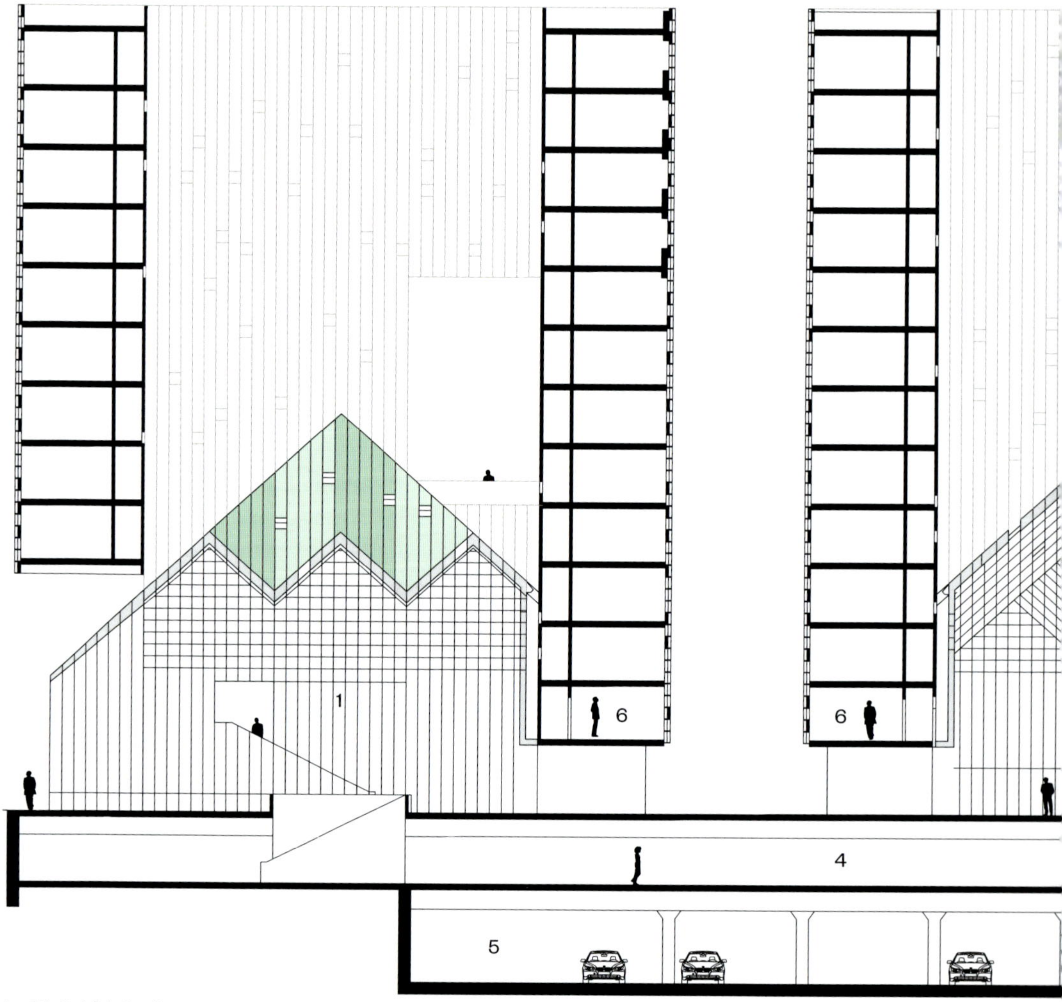

1 Digital fabrication
2 Wood shop
3 Bike hub
4 Materials warehouse
5 Parking
6 Office/studio

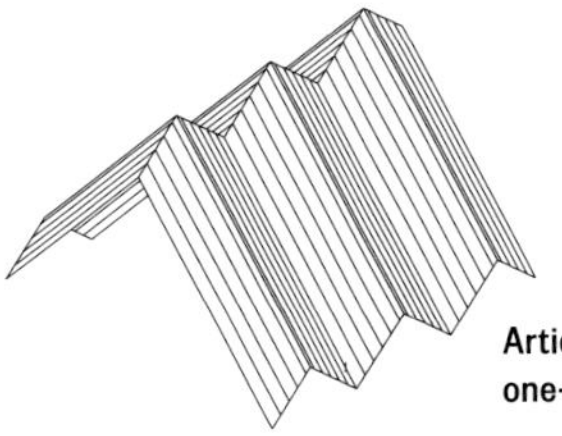

Articulated
one-way vault

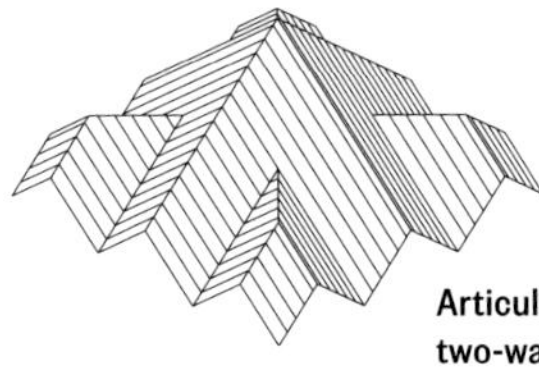

Articulated
two-way vault

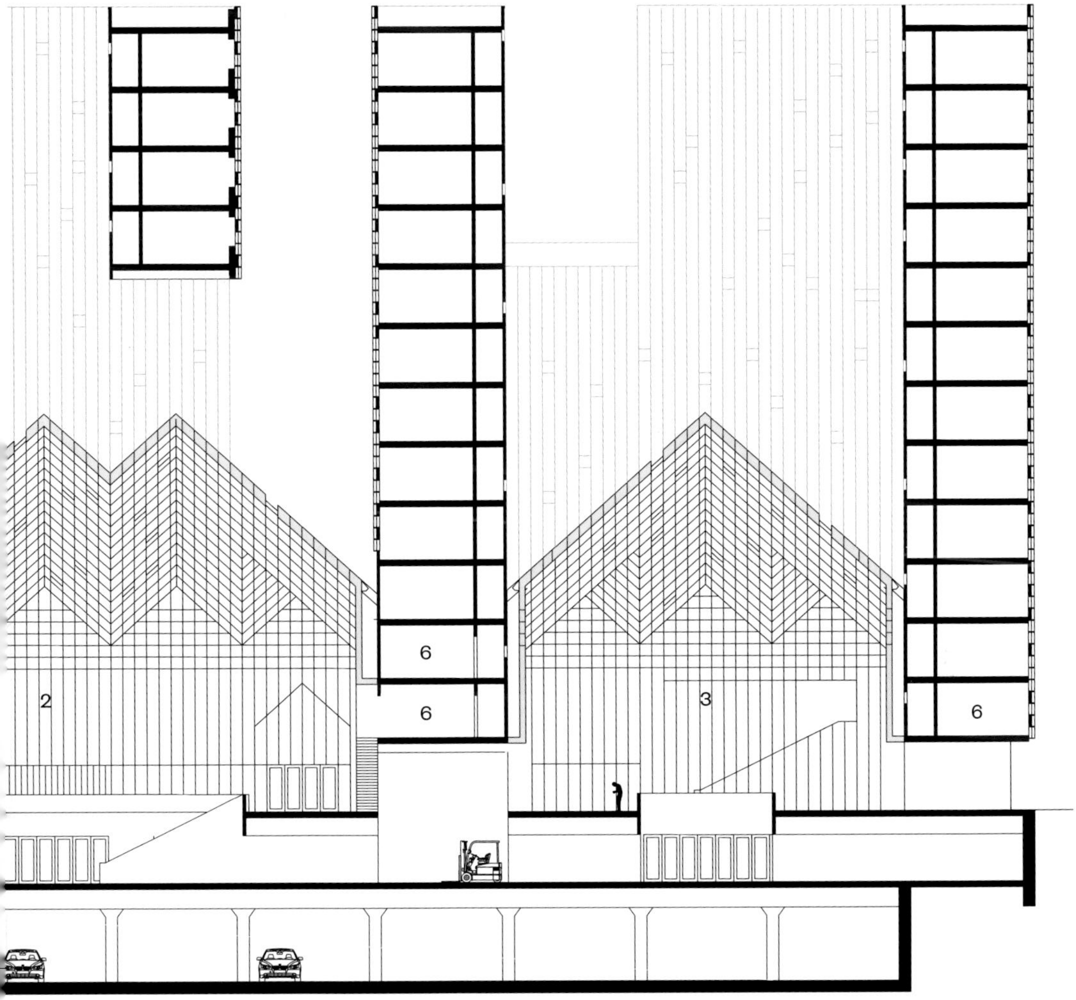

BUILDING SYSTEMS

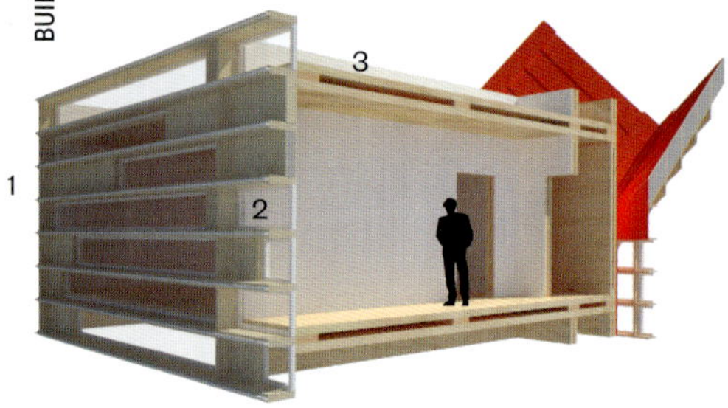

1 Exterior glazing screen
2 Internal thermal window
3 CLT floor system

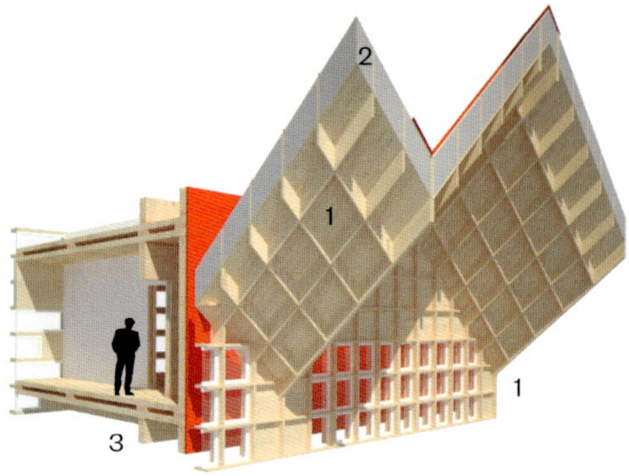

1 Glulam coffer
2 Cellulose insulation
3 CLT vertical support

STRUCTURE

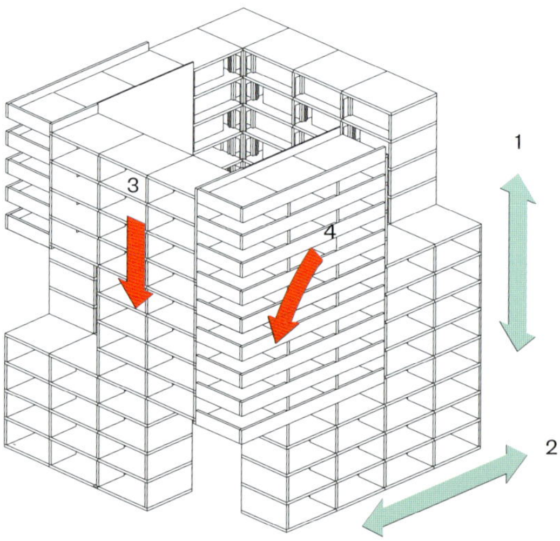

1 Vertical support
2 Floor plates
3 Hanging spans
4 CLT backspan

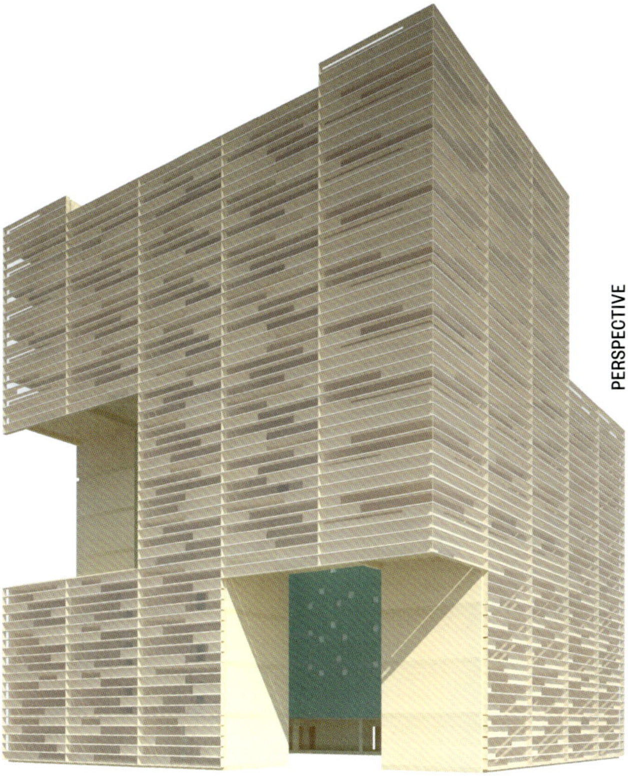

PERSPECTIVE

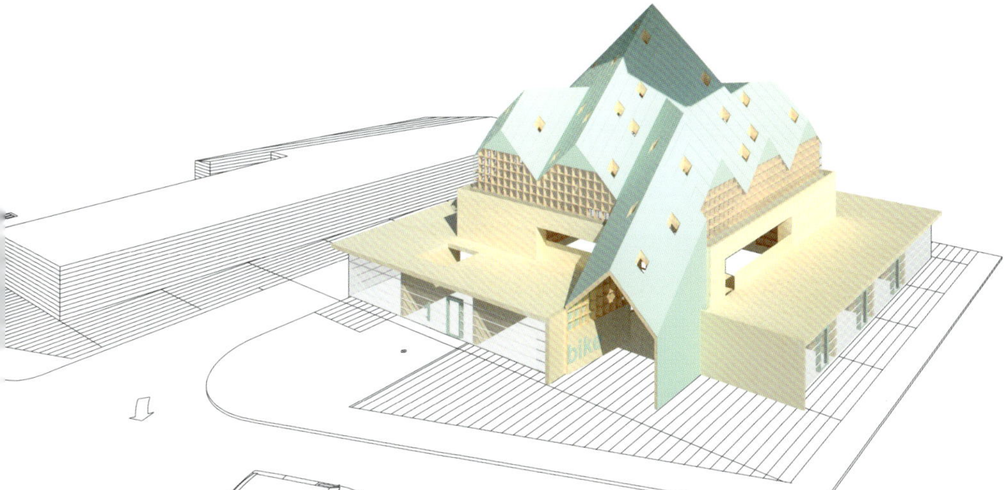

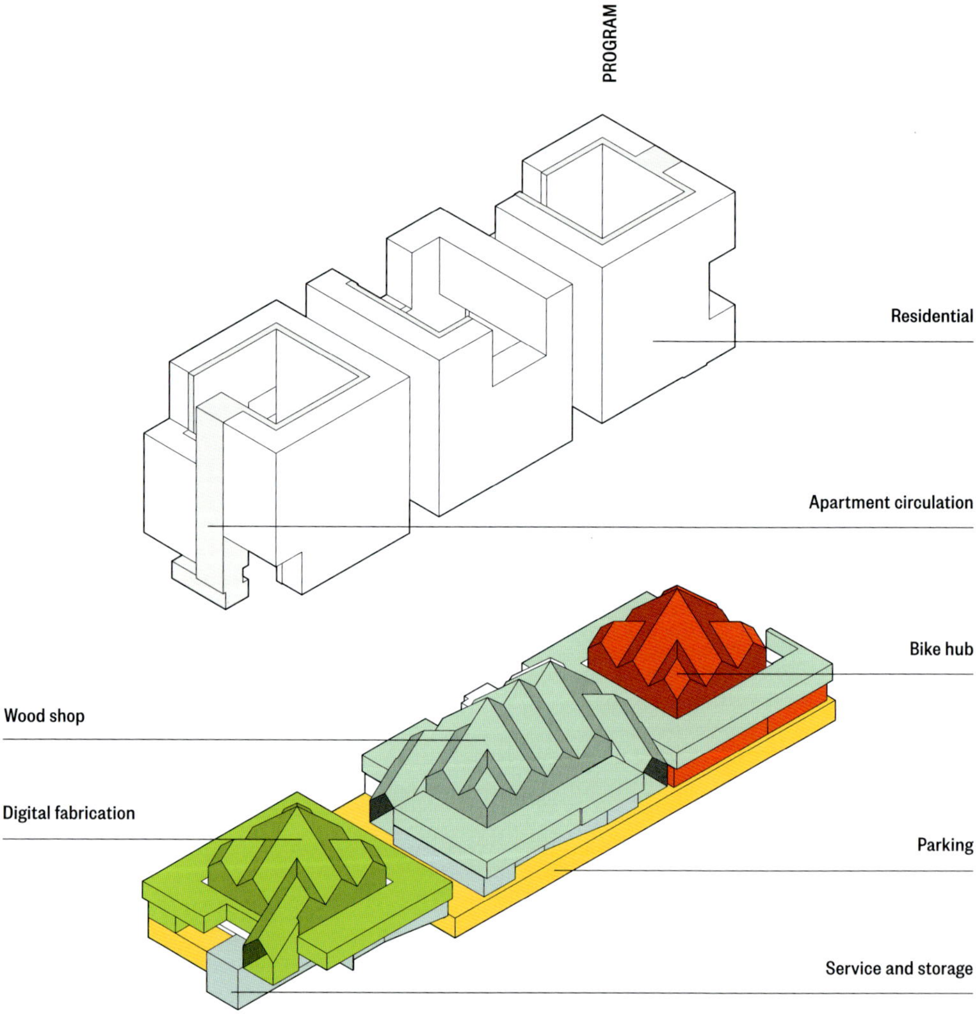
PROGRAM
Residential
Apartment circulation
Bike hub
Wood shop
Digital fabrication
Parking
Service and storage

WORKS

WORKS

3XGRÜN

Atelier PK Architekten

Berlin, Germany

2012

The first realization of a prefabricated timber building prototype stemming from a research project at the Institute for Urban Timber Construction, 3XGRÜN is a multifamily apartment building with garden, balcony, and shared roof deck. The research team developed an urban building typology of up to five stories. The concept allows for flexibility in design as well as in adaptation to existing conditions—infill lots, complete city blocks, detached houses. The key idea is individual prefabrication through user involvement.

The first prototype, in the Florakiez area of Berlin-Pankow, has been realized on two lots. The new building negotiates the varying eave heights, setbacks, and front yards of the neighboring structures, meeting the street with a generous central entrance flanked by two interior stairwells. The thirteen one- and two-story units range from 100 to 200 square meters, and each is oriented toward both the front lawn and the back garden. The units were drawn up with the future owners, as were the shared public areas, the basement with its pellet heating system and extremely energy-efficient technical equipment, and even the facade.

The expression of the apartments is unified on the exterior by overhanging metal bands that mark each floor and at the same time provide solar protection. Between the bands, full-height windows alternate with facade panels according to the interior disposition of the living area. On the third, fourth, and fifth floors, the bands become connected walkways protected by steel guardrails. At ground level, the base of the building is differentiated by wood-faced panels and larger glazed openings.

The structure consists of prefabricated-timber and precast-concrete elements. The partially underground basement, stair cores, fire walls, and ceiling over the ground floor are reinforced concrete; the rest is timber construction. Eighteen-centimeter-thick heavy timber ceilings rest on beams that run along the building's long axis at the facade and stair cores. The beams rest on timber supports. All projections and balconies are cantilevered timber ceilings. The underside of the ceilings is coated with a clear fire-resistant sealant and left exposed so that the timber construction is visible from the outside.

As much as possible, building components were prefabricated. Facade elements consist of insulated timber frames with paintable surfaces and sealant tracks, which came together easily on site. A short construction period and great precision characterize 3XGRÜN, as well as future buildings stemming from the prototype.

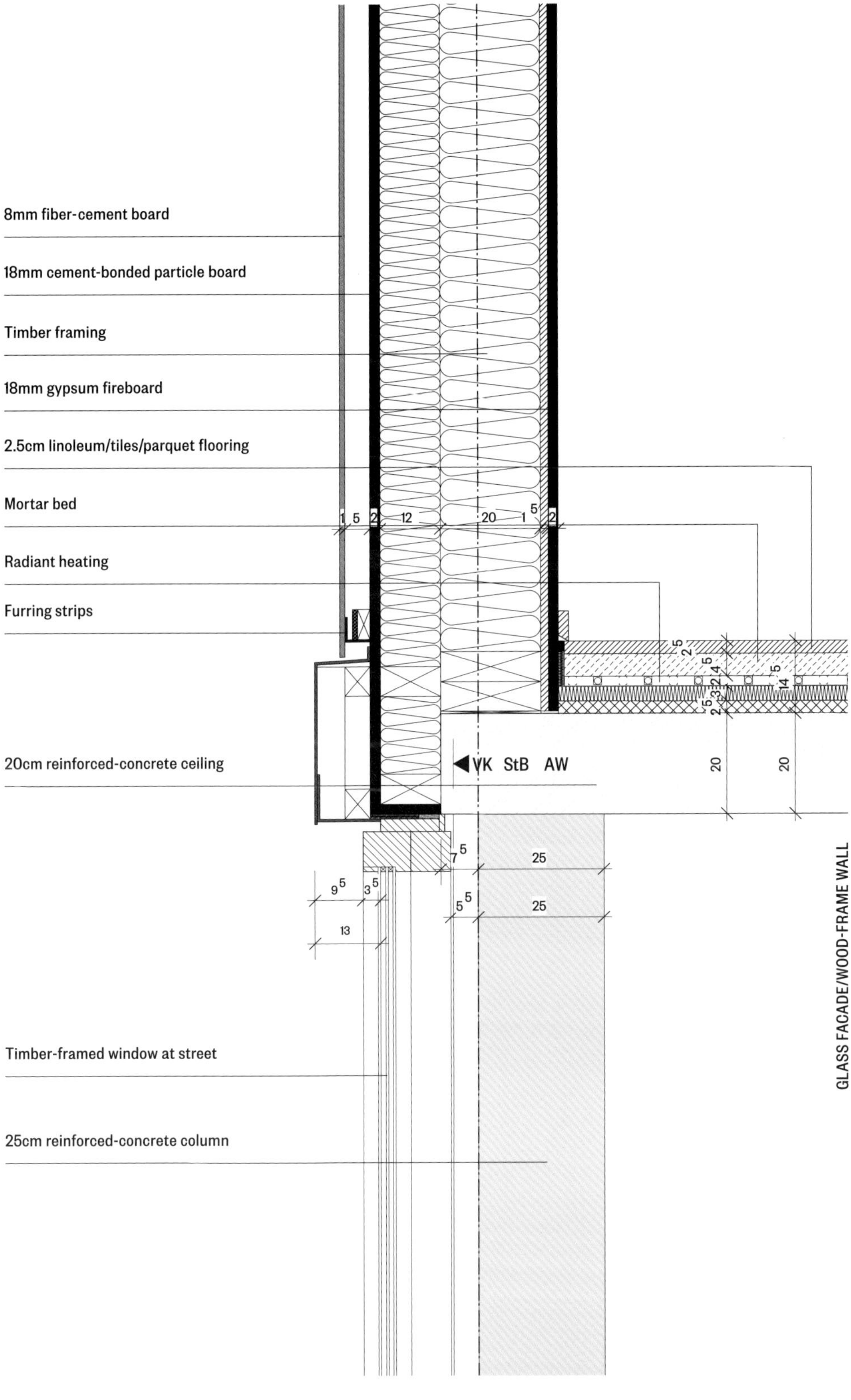

GLASS FACADE/WOOD-FRAME WALL

PLANS

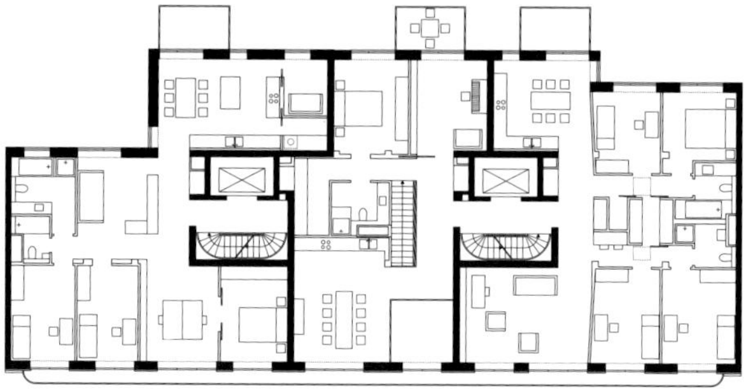

Floor 4

Floor 3

Floor 1

Floor 0

OBER

WORKS

Tamedia

Shigeru Ban Architects

Zurich, Switzerland

2013

The new headquarters for the Swiss media company Tamedia is located in the heart of Zurich. The 1,000-square-meter site, facing the Silh Canal, is positioned within a larger urban block consisting of the main buildings of the group. The new structure occupies the footprint of an earlier edifice but creates continuity with the facades of nearby buildings and takes advantage of the maximum allowed height.

The principal entry to the building is situated in the acute angle formed by Werdstrasse and Stauffacherquai; this will eventually become the main entrance to the complex. The 8,600-square-meter headquarters is seven stories high, with two basement levels.

One of the focal features of the project is the structural system, based entirely on timber. Innovative from both technical and environmental standpoints, the structure also creates a unique visual expression immediately evident on the interior and also in the view from the surrounding city. A fully glazed building skin emphasizes the distinctive wood framework. The low-E glass responds to very strict Swiss energy regulations.

The east facade, which faces the city, also features a full-height intermediate space. It acts as a thermal screen within the general strategy for energy use, but it also offers a singular spatial experience that features lounge areas and vertical links between floors. These "balconies" can be used as informal meeting and rest areas; the facade, a retractable glass window system, can transform these spaces into open-air terraces, reinforcing the relationship between the building and its environment.

tamedia

AXONOMETRIC

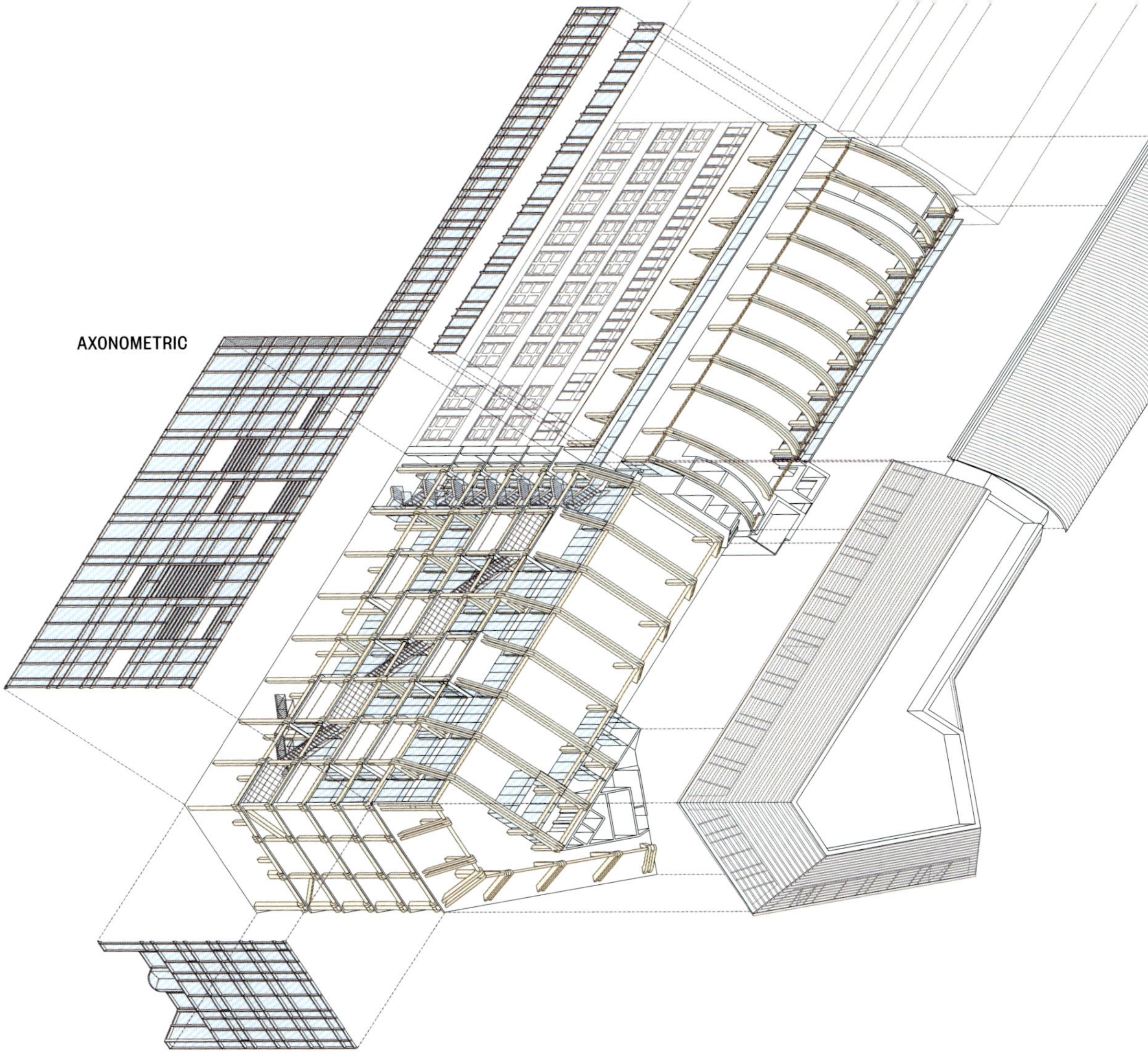

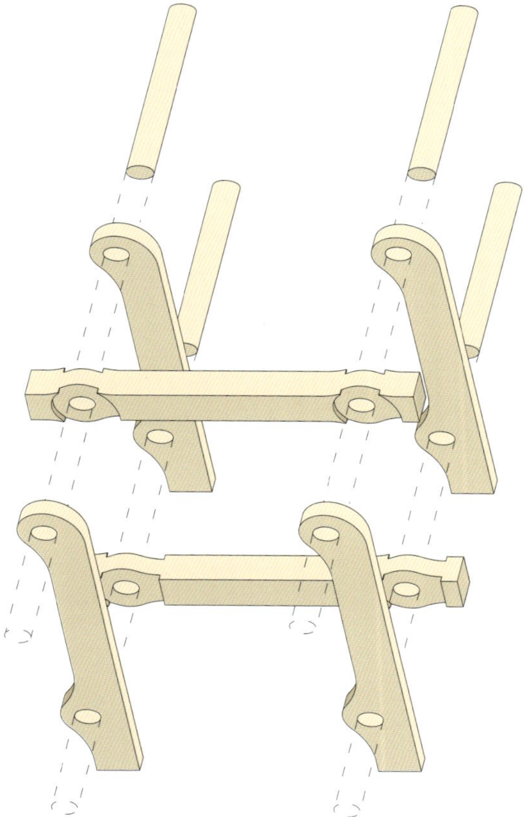

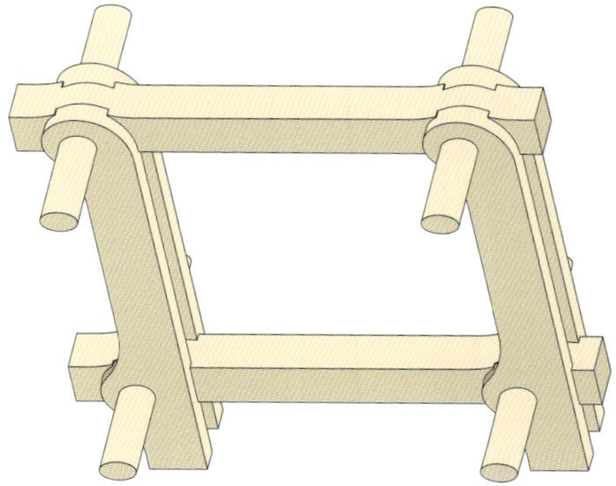

TIMBER DETAIL

SECTION DETAIL

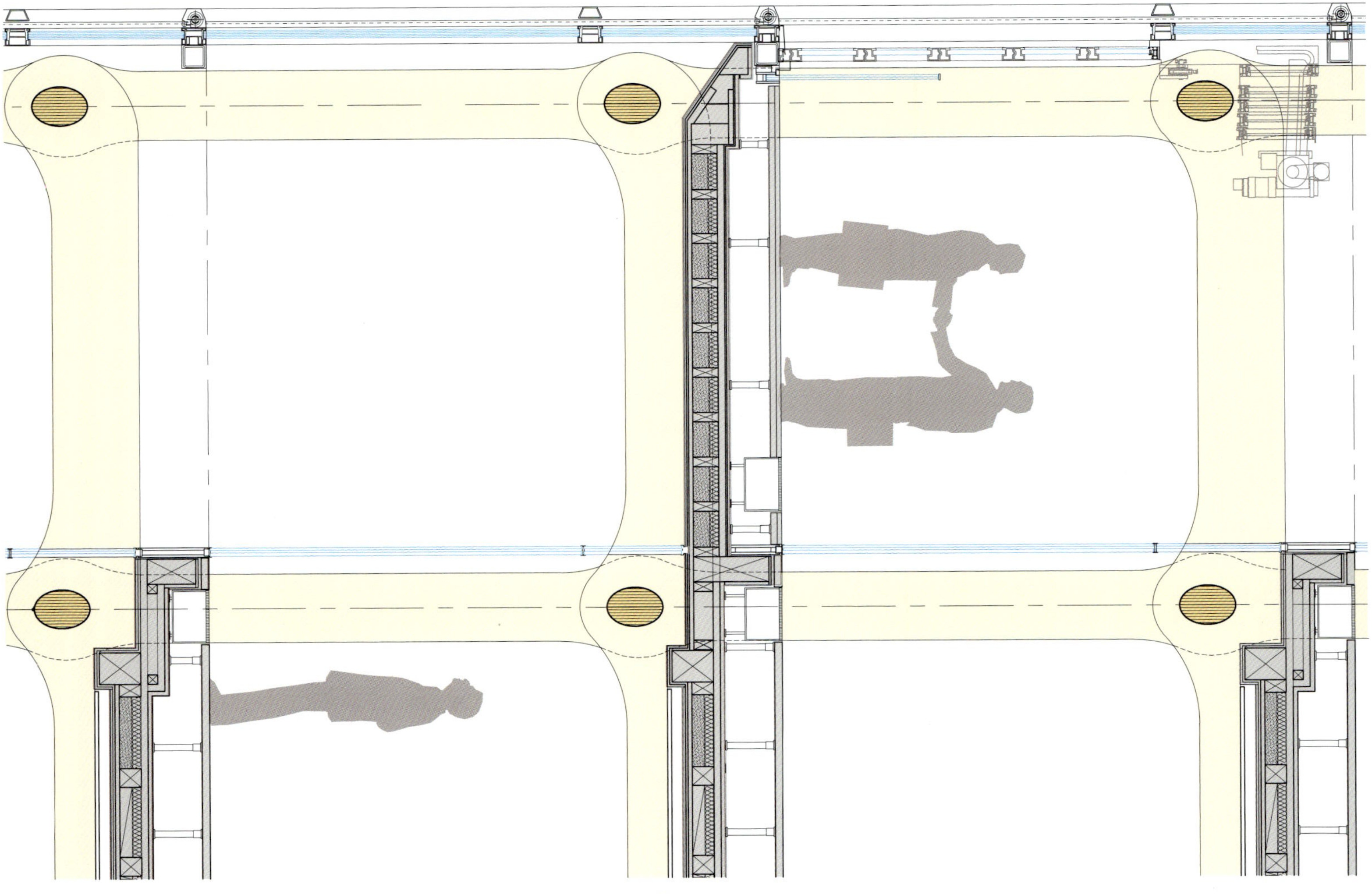

Elm Park

Bucholz McEvoy Architects

Dublin, Ireland

2008

Elm Park consists of 100,000 square meters of office and residential space, along with associated services: hospital, hotel, senior housing, day care, conference center, leisure facilities, and restaurants, all within a richly landscaped park. Buildings on the eight-hectare site are oriented to minimize energy demand and use of generated energy, maximize natural light and ventilation, reduce carbon emissions related to both construction and operation, create connections between activities and people, and provide a district of sufficient density to attract visitors and residents alike.

Buildings are relatively thin and oriented in a north-south direction to optimize access to views and to solar and wind resources. The thermal mass of the buildings mediates internal temperature, lessening the need for mechanical heating and cooling. Building facades are fine-tuned to harness the energy of the prevailing winds. Most of the construction elements of the apartments were prefabricated for speed of construction and quality of finished elements. Pop-out living terraces are actually room extensions. Bathrooms and kitchens are constructed as prefabricated pods, with cladding on timber frames and aluminum face caps to the outside.

In the offices, a combined heat and power system generates electricity and also recycles energy through a waste-heat-to-energy conversion. In the residential buildings, wood pellet boilers supply hot water for heating. An energy management strategy moves energy around according to demand: excess heat can be stored in the swimming pool or used to heat the apartments during the evening and the offices during the day.

Engineered timber is an integral part of the primary structure at Elm Park. It supports the outer layer of the double-skin facade and also binds the fabric of the garden landscape to the vertical plane of the buildings. The high performance of engineered timber over a long building life recommended it over other structural materials. The design of the landscape draws on three typologies prevalent in the Dublin area: mountain, sea, and park.

This comprehensive approach to sustainability produces an environment calibrated to humanity's need for comfort. Elm Park proposes a new type of urban environment in Dublin, one that is firmly stitched into its natural setting, lowers energy demand, and increases the functional potential of its components.

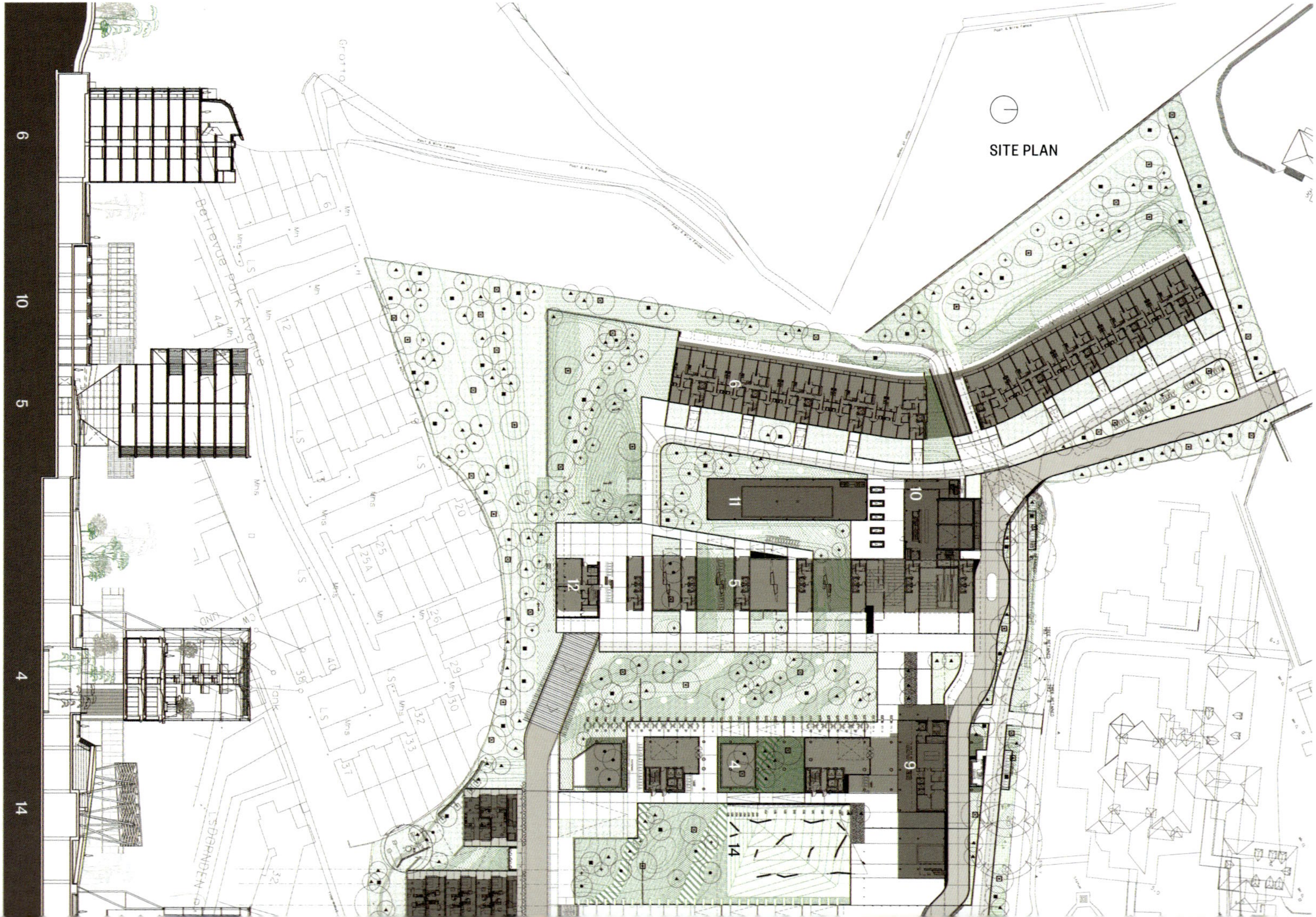
SITE PLAN
6
10
5
4
14
11
12
9
Bellevue Park Avenue
Grotto
Tank

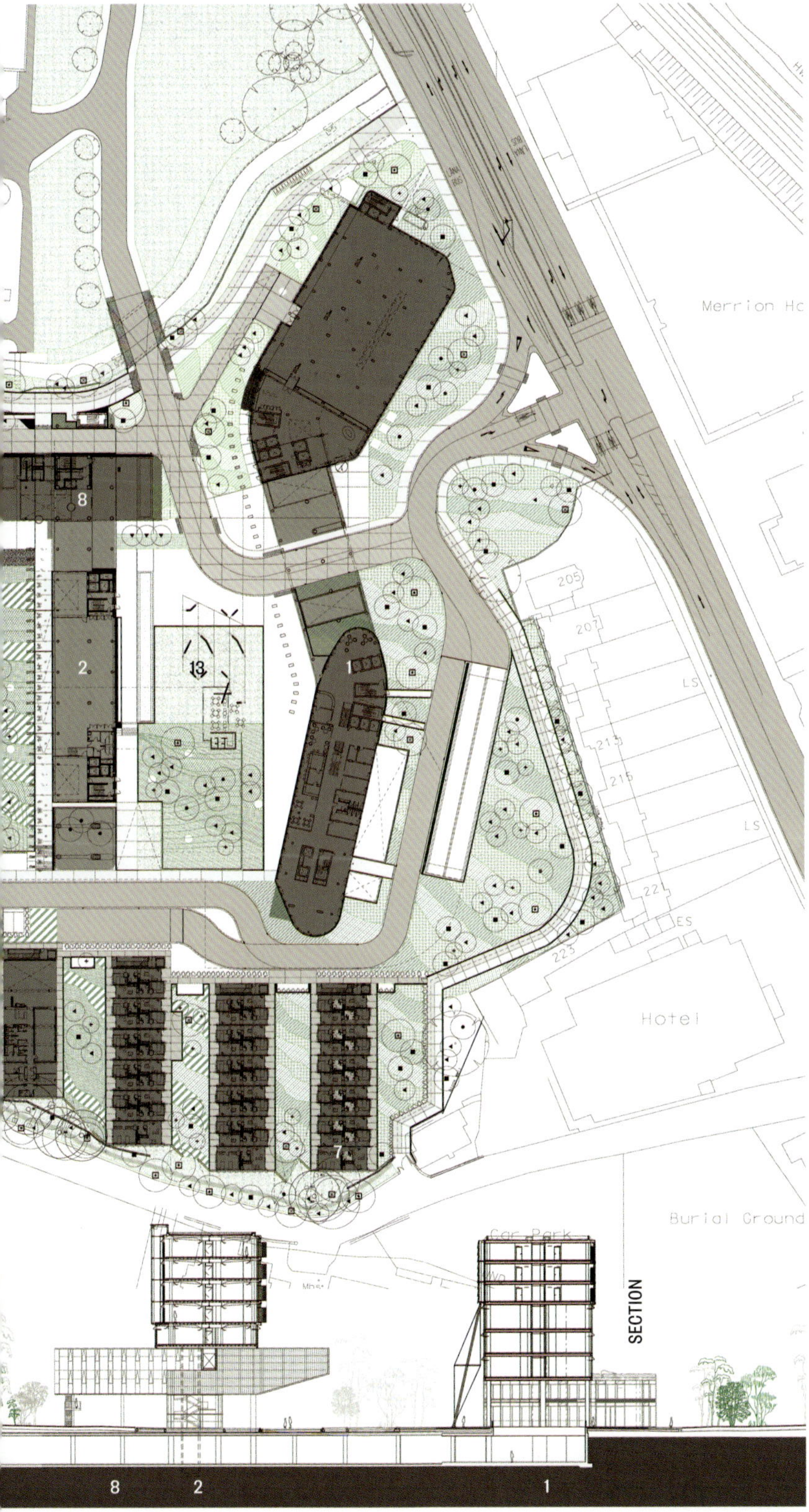

1 Private clinic
2 Office block C
3 Office block B
4 Office block A
5 Residential block 2
6 Residential block 1
7 Senior housing
8 Conference center
9 Restaurant
10 Leisure center
11 Swimming pool
12 Day care
13 Canopy 5
14 Canopy 3

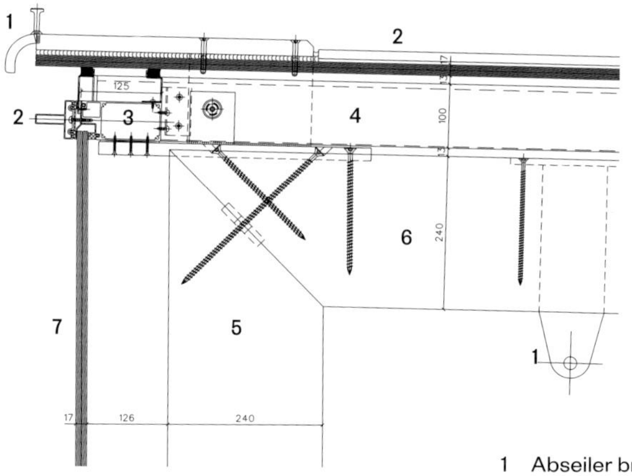

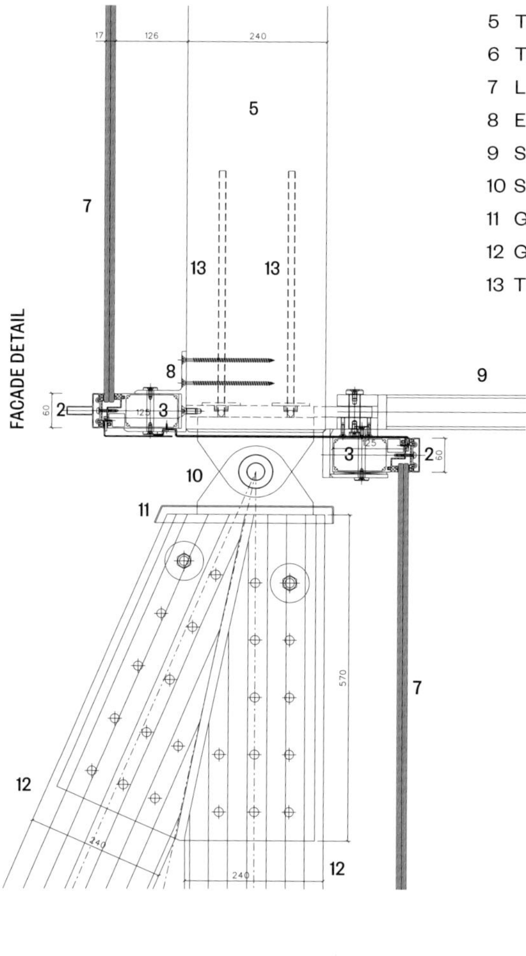

FACADE DETAIL

1 Abseiler bracket
2 Extruded aluminum cover
3 Extruded aluminum transom
4 Extruded aluminum mullion
5 Timber post (Scots pine)
6 Timber beam (Scots pine)
7 Laminated glass
8 Extruded aluminum bracket
9 Strut
10 Steel-pinned joint
11 Galvanized mild steel cover
12 Glue-laminated timber strut (Scots pine)
13 Threaded bar

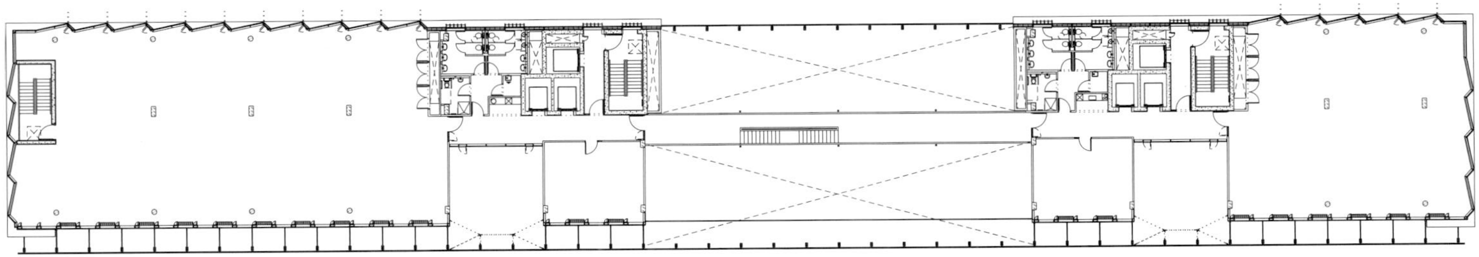

PLAN

Community, Arts, and Sciences Building, Common Ground High School

Gray Organschi Architecture

New Haven, Connecticut

2015

Common Ground High School, an environmental charter school in New Haven, combines urban agriculture and sustainable land-management practices in an innovative curriculum. In addition to the teenagers who attend high school, the facility serves younger children and adults in the afternoons and evenings. The Community, Arts, and Sciences Building and its exterior spaces are woven into the school's fabric of farm buildings, agricultural fields, upland forests, and wetland habitat, a working landscape and outdoor classroom. The building is an environmental exemplar that integrates new ecological concepts and construction technologies in a legible and potentially informative way.

In addition to on-site energy production and storm-water treatment, natural illumination, and passive ventilation, the new building at Common Ground exploits the structural capacities and ecological benefits of wood fiber. It is one of the first buildings in the United States to use cross-laminated timber as its primary structure. Black spruce CLT panels act as the tension surface—and final ceiling finish—in a system of prefabricated stressed-skin assemblies that spans the upper classrooms and circulation spaces. Vertical CLT panels form bearing and shear walls throughout the building; glue-laminated rafters and heavy timber trusses span the large ground-floor multipurpose space. A treated glulam bridge deck on laminated timber piers provides access from the upper campus. Dense cellulose batts superinsulate the airtight enclosure.

One notable benefit of this aggregation of construction biomass is that the building is carbon neutral in its first decade of operation. The carbon sequestered in the building's structural system offsets the annual emissions of 77 cars. An integrated use of renewable materials and low-impact construction enhances the health and ecological function of the immediate site. It also protects more distant productive landscapes, optimizing their biological and hydrological processes so that they may continue to provide valuable environmental services such as clean air, clean water, and a steady supply of renewable building material to cities and, more specifically, to important, forward-thinking institutions like Common Ground High School.

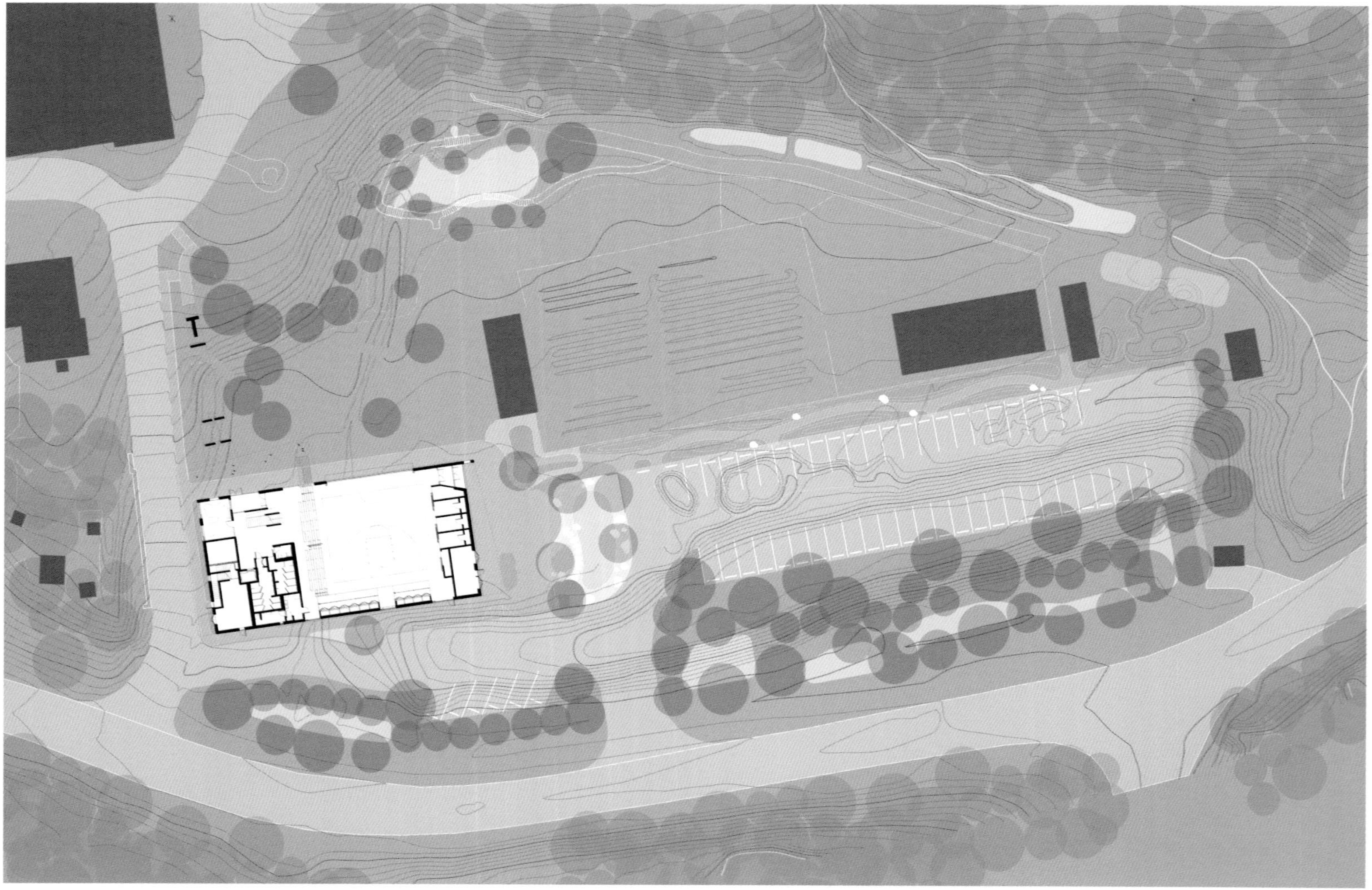

SITE PLAN

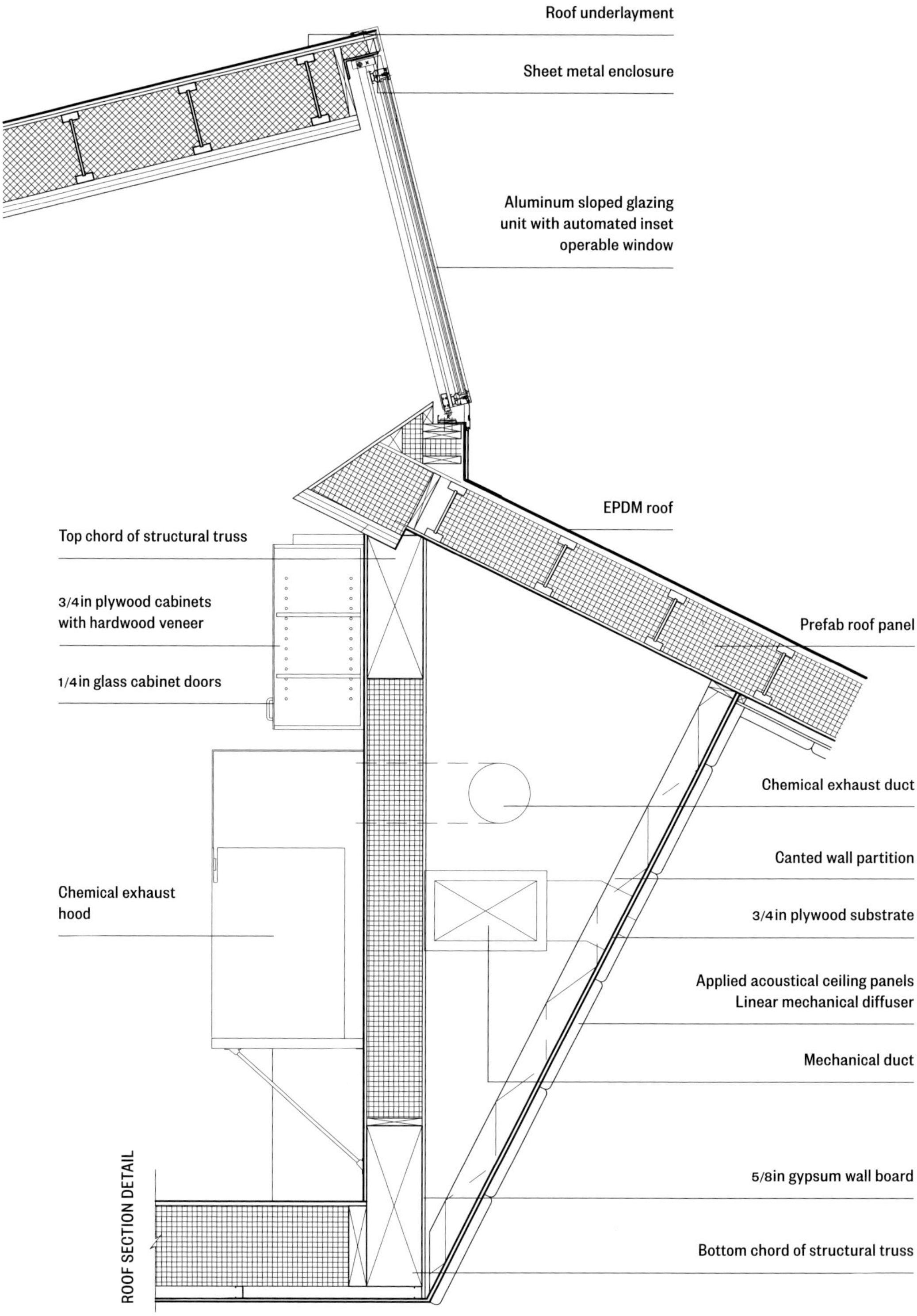

ROOF SECTION DETAIL

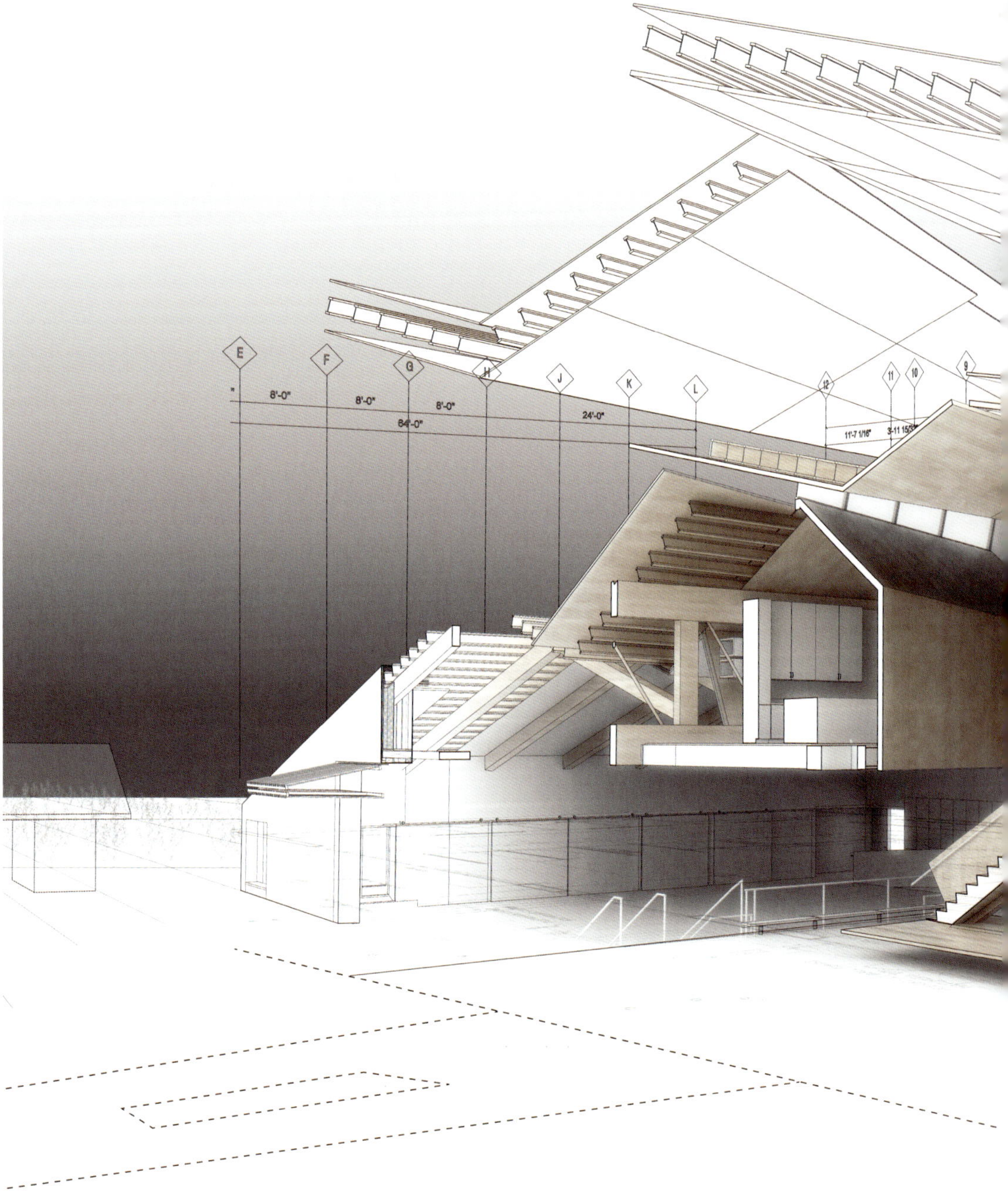
E
F
G
H
J
K
L
12
11
10
9
8'-0"
8'-0"
8'-0"
64'-0"
24'-0"
11'-7 1/16"

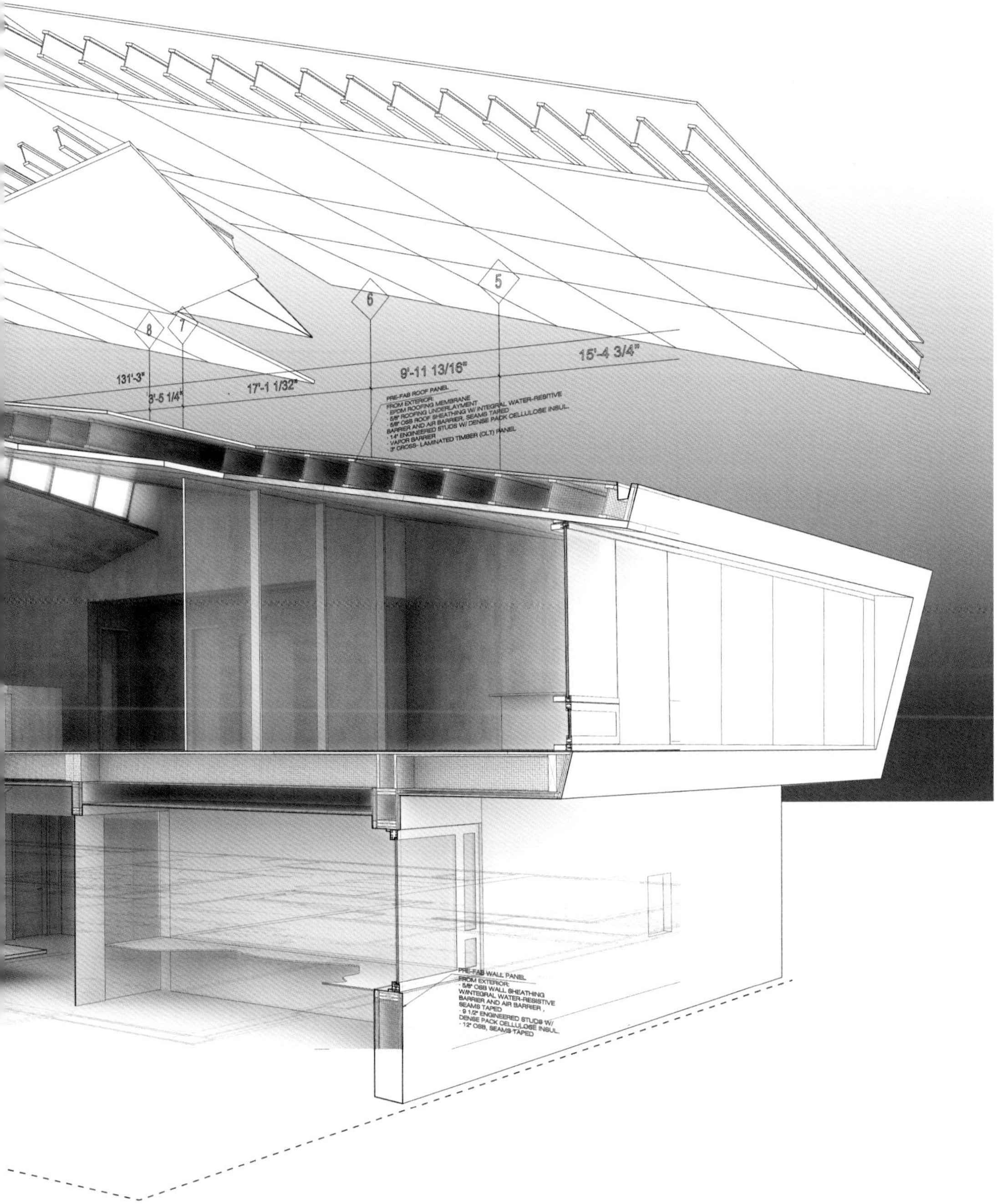
8
7
6
5
131'-3"
3'-5 1/4"
17'-1 1/32"
9'-11 13/16"
15'-4 3/4"
PRE-FAB ROOF PANEL
FROM EXTERIOR:
· EPDM ROOFING MEMBRANE
· 5/8" ROOFING UNDERLAYMENT
· 5/8" OSB ROOF SHEATHING W/ INTEGRAL WATER-RESITIVE
BARRIER AND AIR BARRIER, SEAMS TAPED
· 14" ENGINEERED STUDS W/ DENSE PACK CELLULOSE INSUL.
· VAPOR BARRIER
· 3" CROSS- LAMINATED TIMBER (CLT) PANEL
PRE-FAB WALL PANEL
FROM EXTERIOR:
· 5/8" OSB WALL SHEATHING
W/INTEGRAL WATER-RESISTIVE
BARRIER AND AIR BARRIER ,
SEAMS TAPED
· 9 1/2" ENGINEERED STUDS W/
DENSE PACK CELLULOSE INSUL.
· 12" OSB, SEAMS TAPED

WIDC

WORKS

Wood Innovation and Design Center

Michael Green Architecture

Prince George, British Columbia, Canada

2014

The design for the Wood Innovation and Design Center celebrates timber as one of the world's most beautiful and sustainable building materials. The six-story building, 29.5 meters tall, is a gathering place for researchers, academics, and design professionals interested in generating ideas for innovative uses of wood.

The design incorporates a simple, "dry" structure: systems-integrated floor panels, glulam columns and beams, and mass timber walls, with no concrete above the foundation. The floors are composed of a corrugated arrangement of cross-laminated timber panels. The overlap creates alternating troughs on the floors and ceilings; these are used to incorporate building systems. With this configuration, there is no need to conceal the natural wood with a dropped ceiling. The building core is formed entirely of CLT that is erected in three-story panels.

The design of the project ties into current international trends for an architecture based on timber. The center is a stepping stone to further development of wood-centered building technologies. Durable, simple, flexible, and expandable, the design will drive environmentally responsible architecture that serves as the foundation for new commercial and industrial prospects.

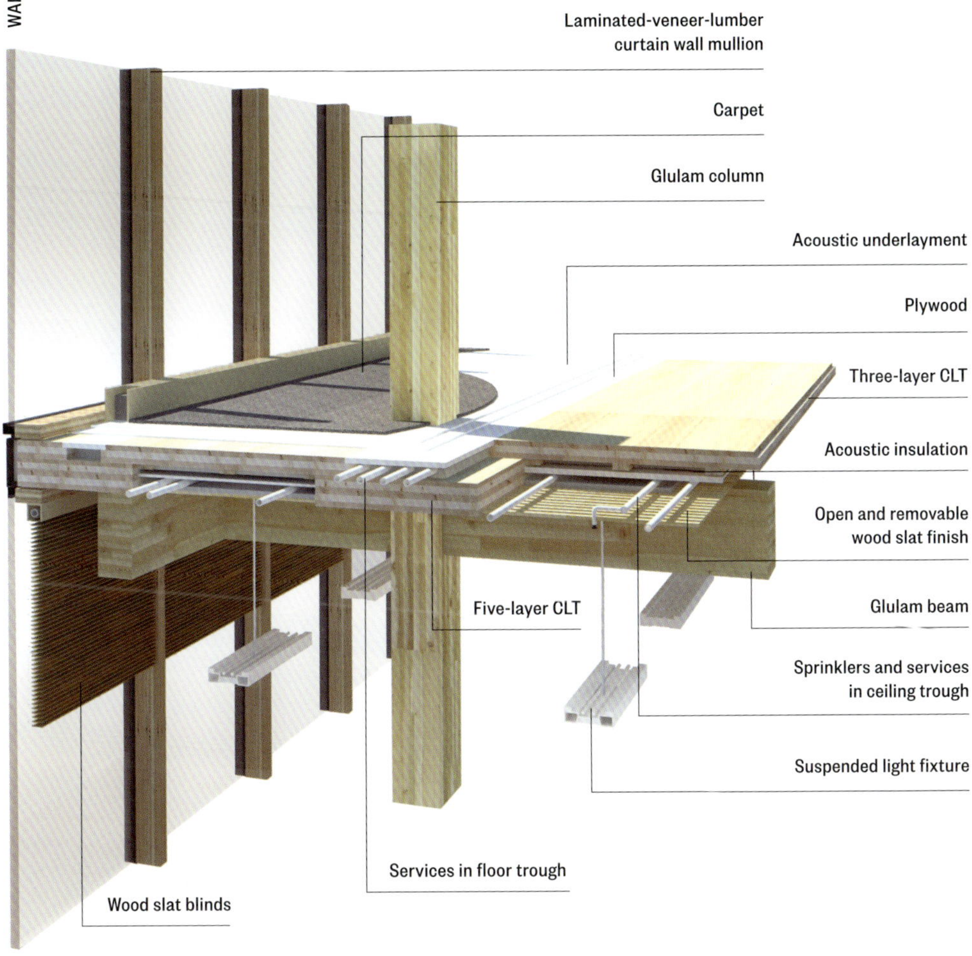
Laminated-veneer-lumber curtain wall mullion
Carpet
Glulam column
Acoustic underlayment
Plywood
Three-layer CLT
Acoustic insulation
Open and removable wood slat finish
Five-layer CLT
Glulam beam
Sprinklers and services in ceiling trough
Suspended light fixture
Services in floor trough
Wood slat blinds

CONSTRUCTION TIMELINE

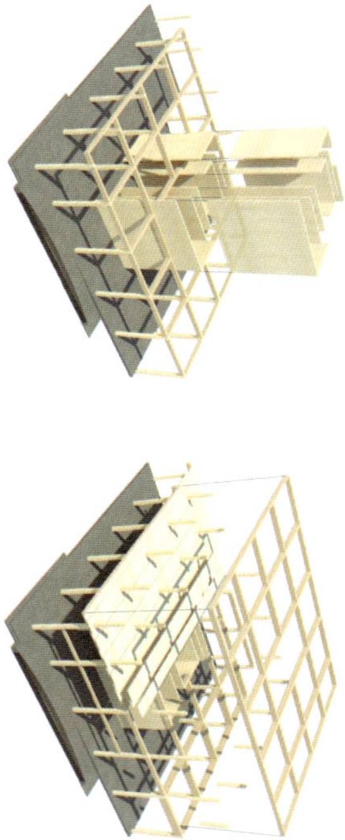

1 Offices
2 Elevator lobby
3 Bathroom

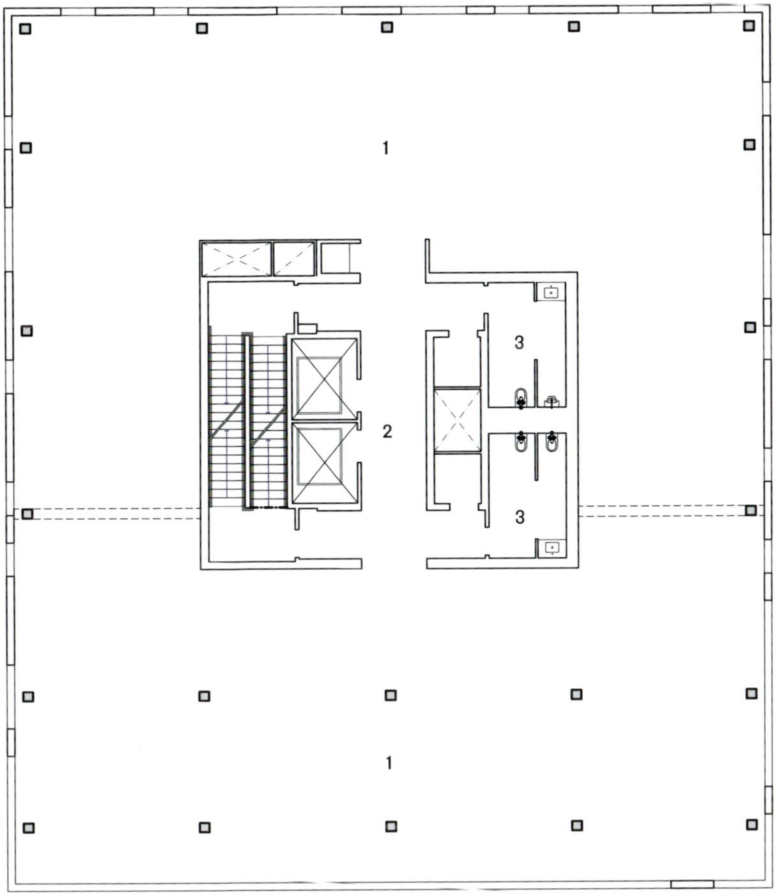

TYPICAL PLAN

WORKS

e3

Kaden + Partner

Berlin, Germany

2008

Located along Esmarchstrasse in Berlin's Prenzlauer Berg area, the e3 apartment building is the first seven-story timber building realized in a large European urban center. Although wood was not exposed on the facade—such an expression would not have fit into the urban context—it was used as a construction and insulation material that offered both high building standards and excellent energy performance.

The living areas are built entirely of wood except for two fire-resistant party walls adjoining the neighboring buildings and cast-in-place concrete cores. The outer walls are composed of load-bearing beams and glulam columns, both 320 by 360 millimeters. They are filled with 160-millimeter solid wood walls.

Heavy timber offers exceptional fire protection. Three strategies overlap to provide fire resistance: short, smoke-free egress paths and the installation of a smoke detection system; the composition of the outer walls, which effectively prevents hard-to-contain cavity fires; and gap-free cladding on all load-bearing and stiffening timber elements. The cladding consists of two layers of eighteen-millimeter gypsum board; once spackled, it is a finished surface ready to be painted.

The timber elements were produced using industrial methods under supervised conditions in a climate-regulated facility. This method of execution, carried out with rigorous quality control, made possible a construction period of only nine months.

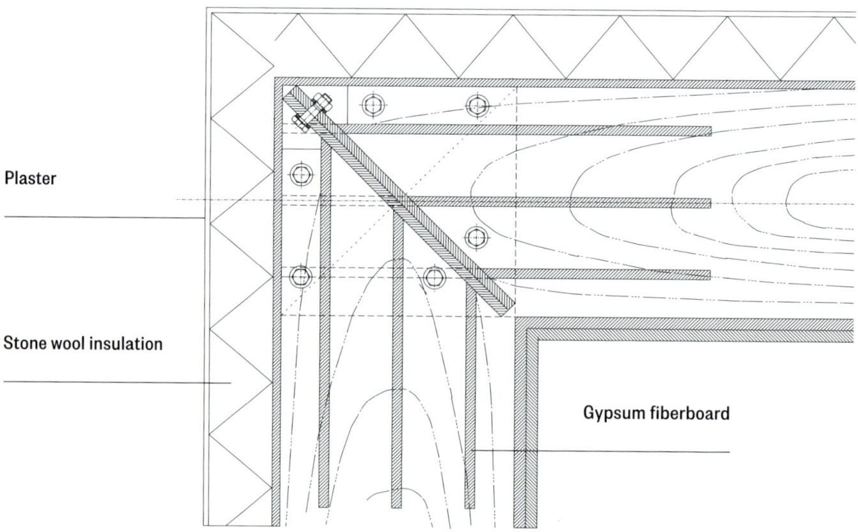

TIMBER CONNECTION DETAIL

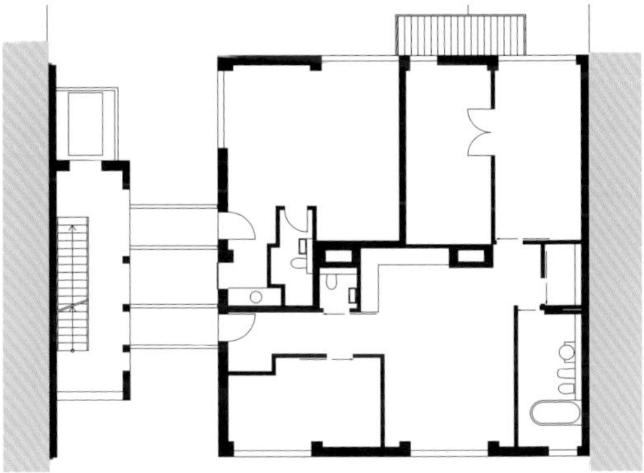

Floor 2

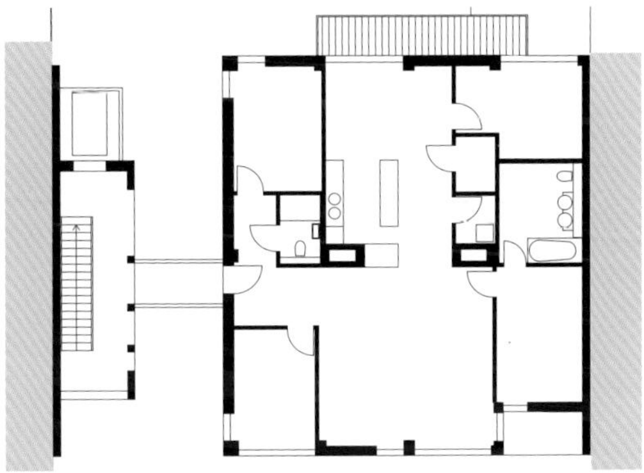

Floor 6

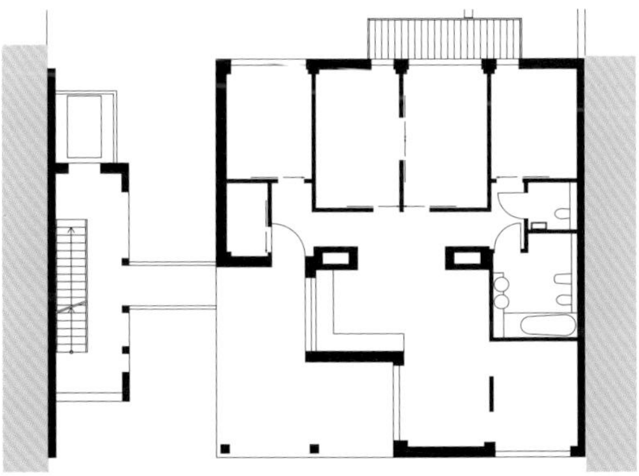

Floor 1

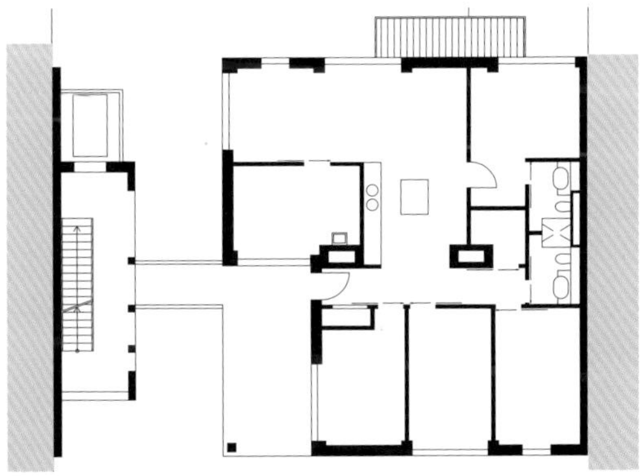

Floor 4

WORKS

Illwerke Zentrum Montafon

Architekten Hermann Kaufmann ZT

Vandans Bludenz, Vorarlberg, Austria

2013

The Illwerke Zentrum Montafon, an office building constructed by means of a wood-hybrid system, accommodates various functions for a series of hydropower plants: control for energy generation, engineering, infrastructure, and administration. Known as LifeCycle Tower, the modular, flexible, wood-hybrid building system has many advantages: it minimizes resource and energy use, has an improved carbon-dioxide balance, and can be constructed quickly and precisely. All building components, including energy supply, are individually configured and optimized.

The body of the building, 120 meters long and with an area of 10,000 square meters, extends partially into an artificial lake on the site. Two access towers and the ceiling of the ground floor are reinforced concrete. The LCT components, including facades, were built in only six weeks. In the LCT system, the load-bearing members in large-volume wood construction remain exposed. Wood-concrete composite elements are carried on glued wood supports integrated into the facade. These supports are held by steel carriers atop a series of reinforced-concrete columns along the central axis. The consistent skeleton offers high flexibility. The wood-concrete hybrid ceiling, an advanced fire apron by the facade, and a sprinkler system ensure fire protection.

LCT construction is based on a high degree of prefabrication and remains adaptable over its full life cycle. It allows custom internal layouts, and external facades can be designed according to what is required within. Here the facades consist of a strict grid of canopy (providing shade and weather protection), wood spandrel, and glazing. Building technology is used sparingly and in a targeted manner. Energy needs for the office building are met by the exhaust heat of one of the power plants; a heat-pump system meets cooling demands.

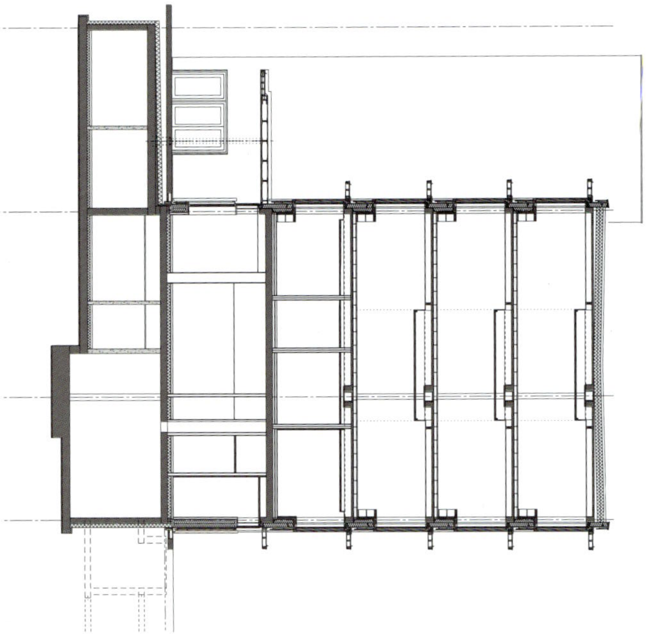

SECTION

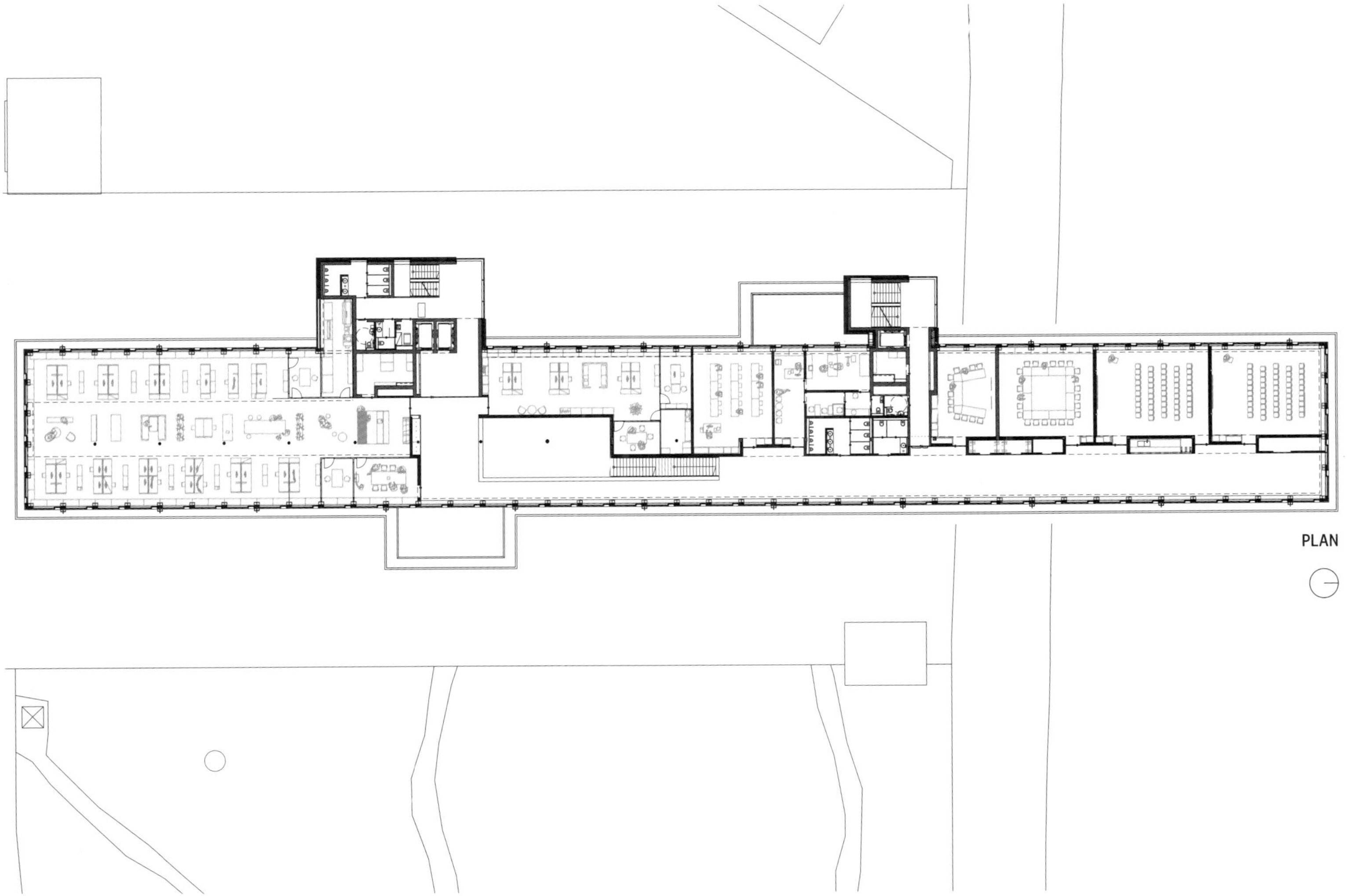
PLAN

SECTION THROUGH FACADE

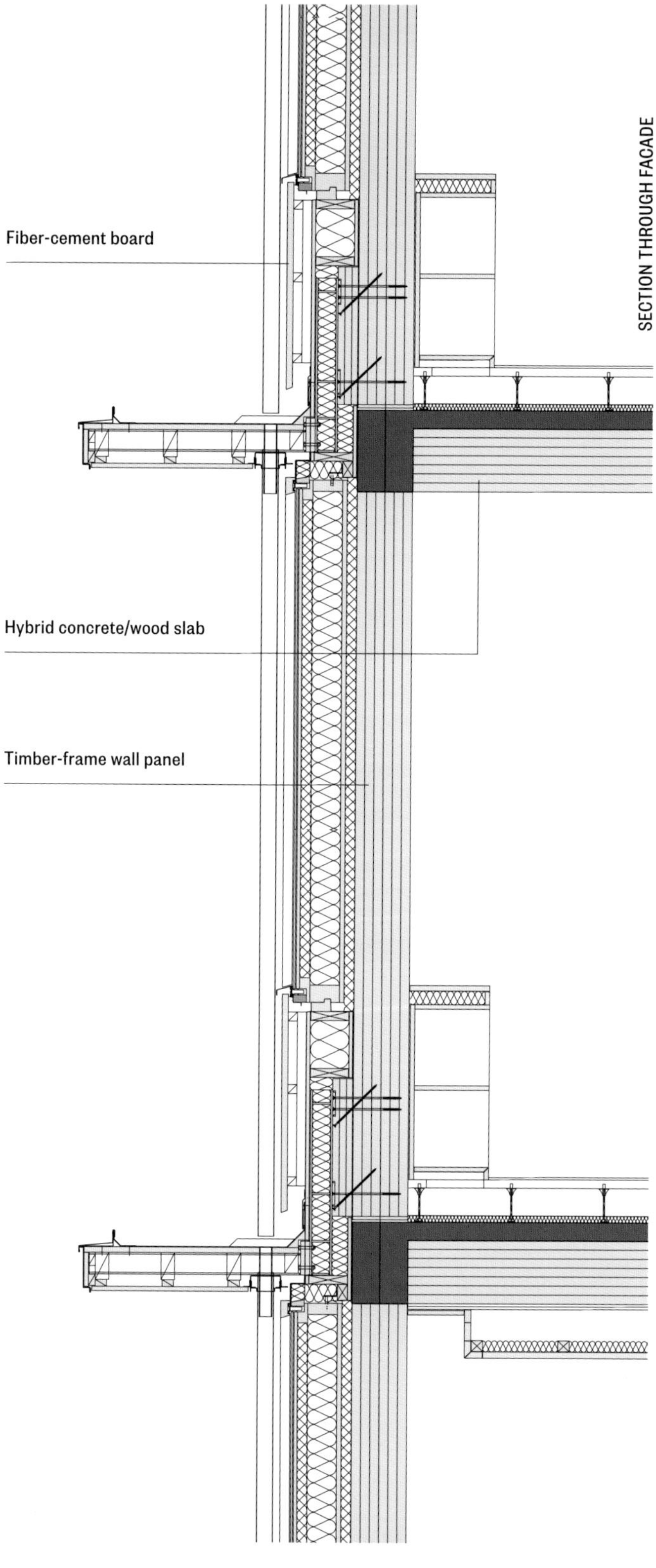

WORKS

Bullitt Center

Miller Hull Partnership

Seattle, Washington

2013

The six-story, 52,000-square-foot Bullitt Center is the first urban mid-rise commercial structure in the United States to target the goals of the Living Building Challenge, a building certification program intended to define advanced sustainability. From design to interactive resource center to new community green space, the Bullitt Center educates its users on green building and urban sustainability. The lower floor of the building houses the Center for Energy and Urban Ecology, with a resource library, classrooms, exhibition space, and research laboratory. Functional elements also serve as interpretive displays, explicating sustainable design in architecture, energy use, material sourcing, government policy, and financing.

The building was conceived as a prototype to demonstrate and inform state-of-the-art sustainable design for future building projects. Every material and building system was evaluated on its contribution to the ultimate goal of net-zero energy use and to ensure that common environmental toxins were not present. Advanced photovoltaic technology provides on-site renewable energy generation. Water needs are met by means of harvested rainwater. Interior work spaces are naturally illuminated and ventilated. The adjacent street has been transformed into green space. Storm-water runoff is retained on site—via native plant restoration, bioswales, and pervious pavement—protecting the health of Puget Sound.

The six-story podium structure has four floors of wood over two stories of reinforced concrete. The Douglas fir glulam beams and columns were joined with simple and efficient custom-designed bucket connectors. Finished to an industrial appearance grade, the structural members were left exposed, revealing the material and avoiding volatile-organic-compound-containing paints and finishes. The heavy timber frame updates a tradition of building in Seattle, where there are many older wood buildings that have lasted through fires, earthquakes, and more than a hundred years of use.

Timber is an apt material choice because one of the goals of the center is to contribute to a regional design vernacular, one informed by the culture and tuned to the environment. The abundance of wooded areas in the Pacific Northwest has fostered extensive timber construction in the region. In addition to its environmental benefits, wood can be considered a local material. Here it has been harvested from responsibly managed forests: all wood used in the Bullitt Center is certified to standards set by the Forest Stewardship Council.

SECTION

WORKS

Sneek Bridge

ONIX AchterboschZantman Kunstwerke

Sneek, The Netherlands

2008

This bridge, which spans the A7 motorway, connects two districts of Sneek, a city of about 33,000. Its form and materials are based on both historic precedents and advanced technologies, capitalizing on the latest innovations in timber construction. Responsible and sustainable, a fusion of infrastructure, construction, art, and architecture, the bridge establishes a new marker for the city.

The bridge is built of Accoya wood, an acetylated wood produced in a factory in Arnhem. The acetylation process reduces the ability of wood to absorb water, making it almost imperishable. The bridge consists of two wooden trusses that are coupled at the center, ensuring great stability. The arched form was derived from optimizing the cross section of the bridge to accommodate traffic. The bridgehead on one side is a green dike element; on the other side, a concrete span that bridges a waterway.

The design of the bridge is both recognizable and new to Sneek. The contours recall the traditional cheese-cover farmhouses of the district of Friesland; the construction alludes to the building expertise of the old city; the wooden beams evoke the history of shipbuilding in Sneek, which has long been known as a center of water recreation.

The bridge, the first uncovered wooden span in the heaviest load class, serves cars, pedestrians, and cyclists. For motorists on the A7, it designates the interface between motorway and city; for travelers on the bridge, the gateway between city center and suburbs.

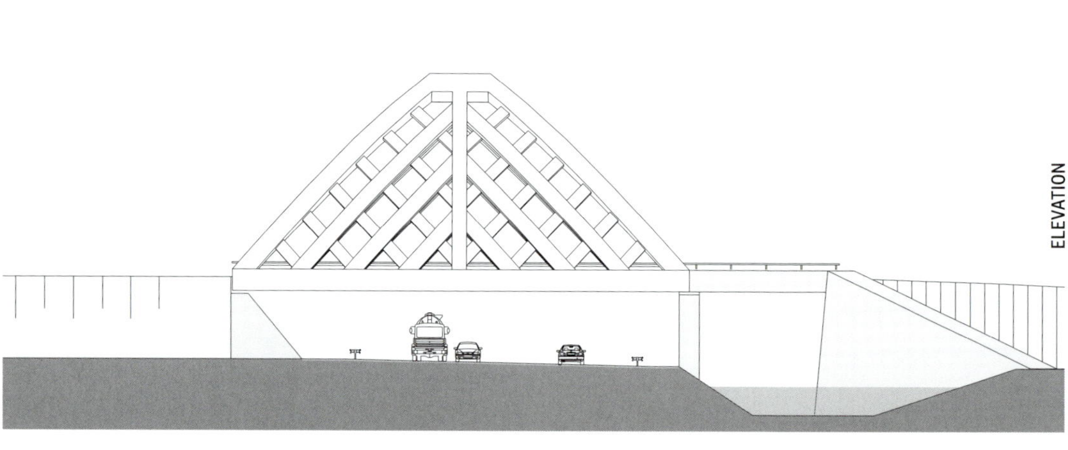

ELEVATION

SITE PLAN

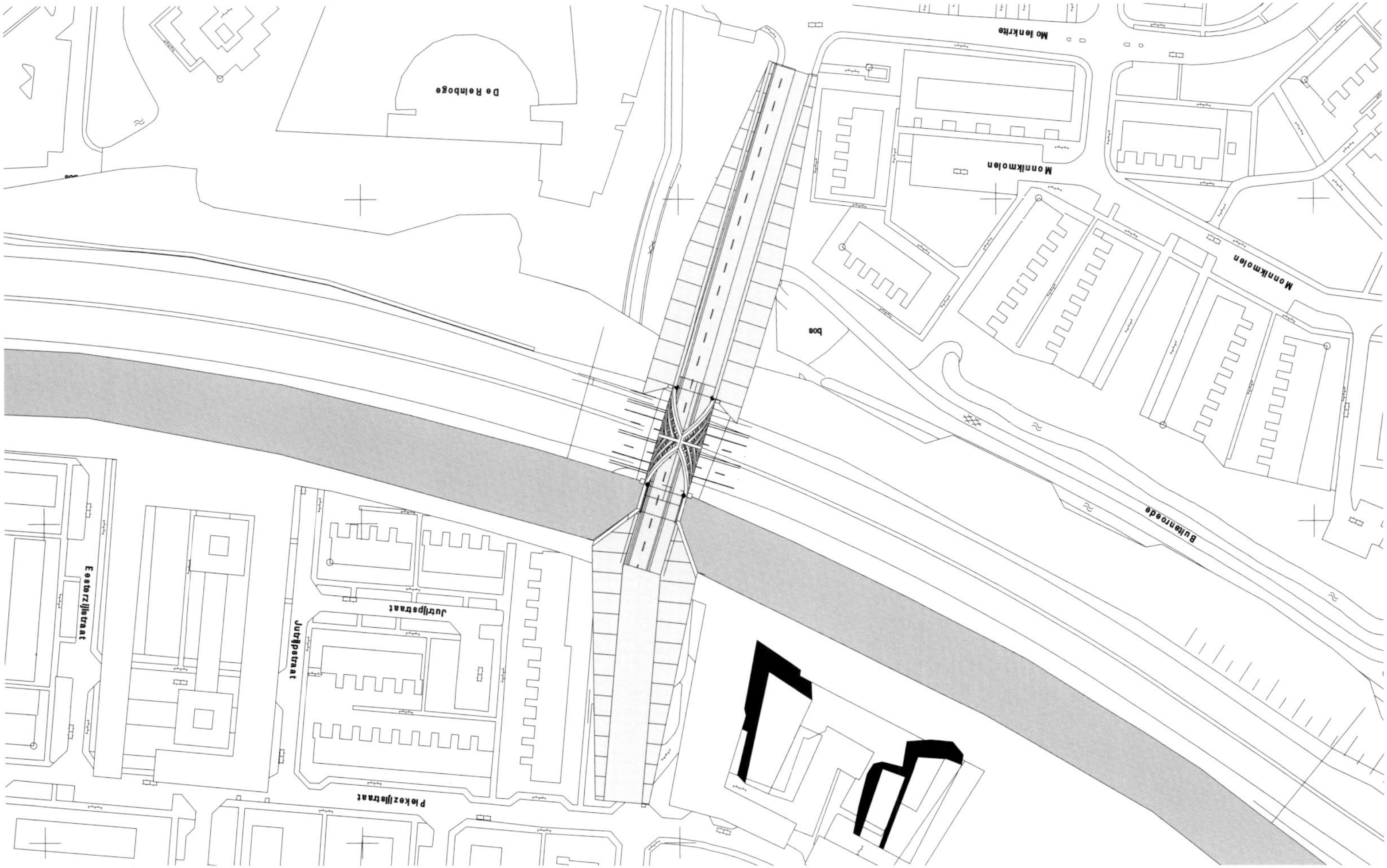
De Reinboge
Molenkrite
Monnikmolen
Monnikmolen
bos
Buitenroede
Eesterzijlstraat
Jutrijpstraat
Jutrijpstraat
Piekezijlstraat

UBC
Earth Sciences Building

Earth Sciences Building, University of British Columbia

Perkins + Will

Vancouver, Canada

2012

Located on the Vancouver campus of the University of British Columbia, the Earth Sciences Building brings together several departments of science, furnishing teaching and research spaces that put science on display while enhancing the public realm of the campus. Wood provides the primary structure of the office wing, offsetting the energy-intensive laboratory functions; the research labs occupy a concrete wing. The facility is the largest solid-wood-panel building and also the largest application of cross-laminated timber in North America to date.

The building plays an important role in reinforcing pedestrian engagement along UBC's Main Mall. The ground level mirrors the Beaty Biodiversity Museum across the mall, creating a museum precinct on campus. The eastern corridor of the building serves as an extension of the Pacific Museum of the Earth, providing a display gateway to this science- and engineering-focused area of the campus.

An interior atrium straddles an existing campus walkway, directing pedestrians into the building and exposing the science taking place inside the structure to the greater campus community. The atrium contains a free-floating staircase made of a seamless folding "ribbon" of rigid glulam stringers. A CLT canopy wraps three sides of the building to provide rain cover. It extends from the interior, where it forms the ceiling finish for the museum and café, to the exterior.

Complying with British Columbia's Wood First Initiative, which aims to promote the use of timber from the province, the Earth Sciences Building incorporates into the main structure prefabricated CLT, laminated-strand lumber, and glue-laminated engineered wood products. The project sets a new standard of performance and innovation in heavy timber construction and demonstrates the efficient use of modern engineered timber for a demanding institutional program.

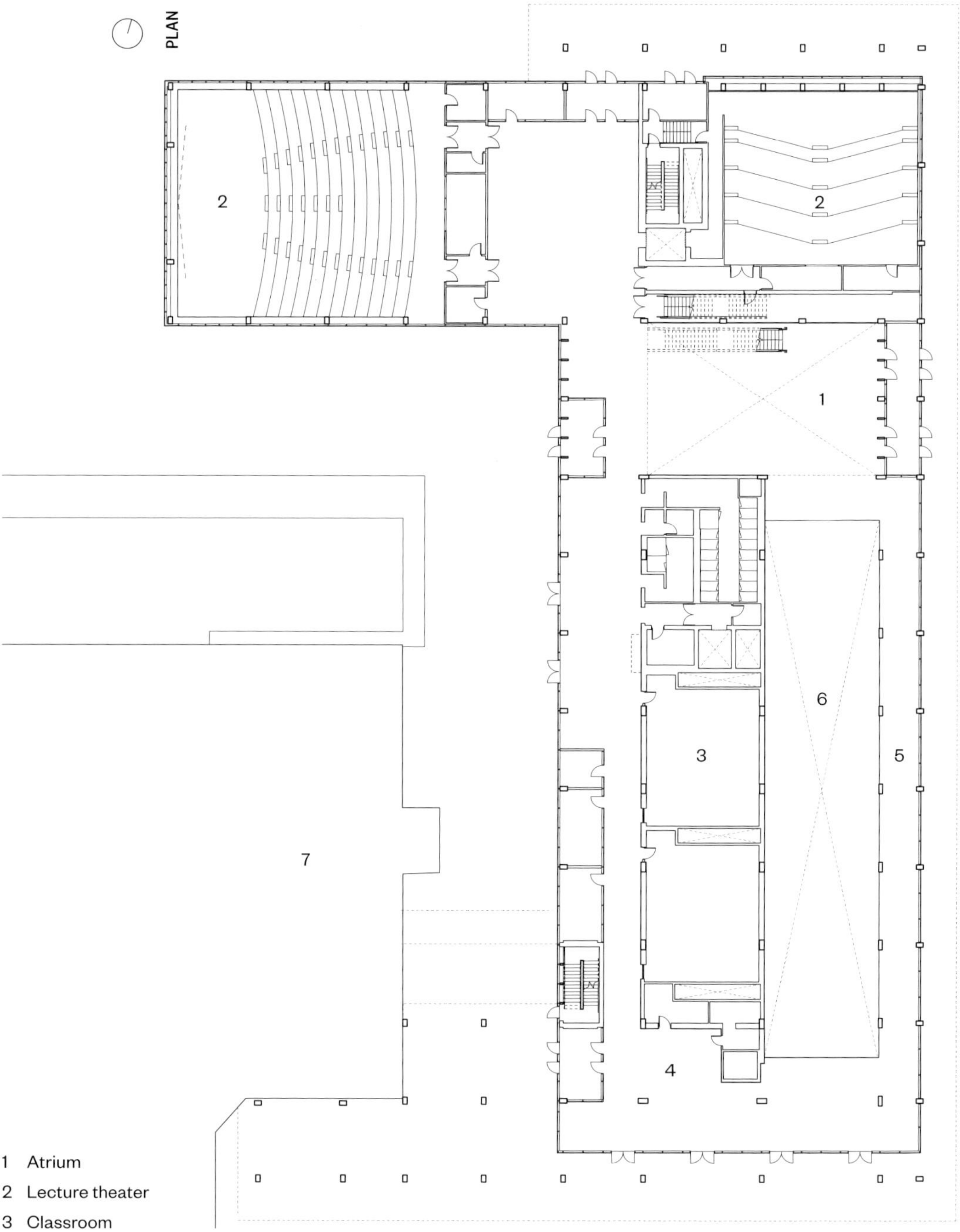

1 Atrium
2 Lecture theater
3 Classroom
4 Café
5 Pacific Museum of the Earth
6 High-headroom laboratories
7 Earth, Ocean, and Atmospheric Sciences Building

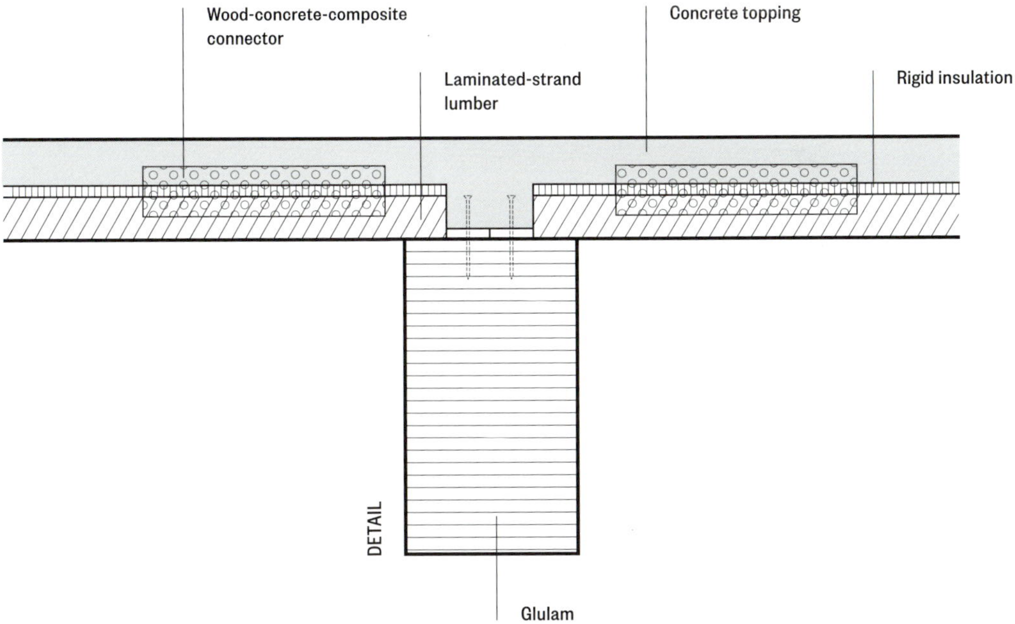
Wood-concrete-composite connector
Laminated-strand lumber
Concrete topping
Rigid insulation
DETAIL
Glulam

SECTION

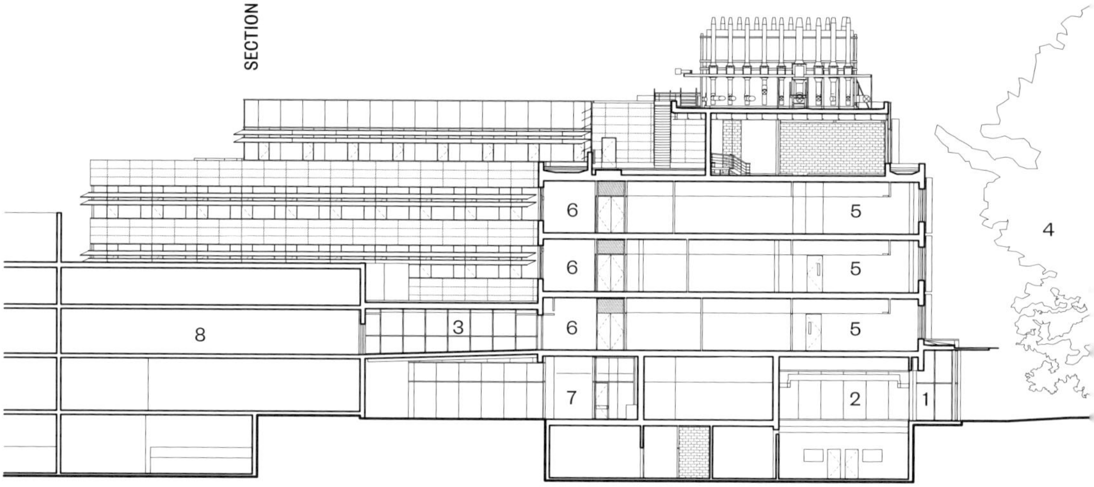

1 Pacific Museum of the Earth
2 High-headroom laboratories
3 Bridge link to Earth, Ocean, and Atmospheric Sciences Building
4 Main Mall
5 Research lab
6 Office
7 Common space
8 Earth, Ocean, and Atmospheric Sciences Building

LUNDIN EXP

ON COMPLEX

WORKS

Soccer Center, Saint-Michel Environmental Complex

Saucier + Perrotte Architectes/ Hughes Condon Marler Architects

Montreal, Canada
2014

This new soccer center is within Montreal's Saint-Michel Environmental Complex, a park under construction on the site of the former Miron Quarry, and along Papineau Avenue, one of the city's major thoroughfares. The form of the building emerges from the artificial topography of the park: it was conceived as a mineral stratum that recalls the geological nature of the site. This mineral layer is articulated as a continuous roof that cantilevers over the entry plaza, passes over an interior soccer field, and folds down and extends to the ground to become spectator seating for a future outdoor field. The stratum is a singular feature that ensures the unity of the soccer center over different programs and construction phases.

The roof is supported by a seemingly arbitrary lattice suspended over the site. The primary structure, consisting of thirteen-foot glulam beams, is braced and to an extent masked by the secondary structure, consisting of four-foot glulam beams. This framework creates an interior space 50 feet high, ensuring optimal views of not only the soccer field but the park outside. The 136,000-square-foot building is anticipated to receive LEED Gold certification.

The internal organization of the soccer center takes advantage of the linearity of the site as well as the needs of players, spectators, and park visitors. The transparency of the building promotes a sense of openness and furnishes an inviting atmosphere for soccer enthusiast and community member alike. Support areas—administrative offices, locker rooms, training room, multipurpose room, and cafeteria—are embedded in a berm along Papineau Avenue. This site-specific accommodation generates an elevated pedestrian path and also preserves the existing trees. A series of "crystals" emerges from the augmented landscape to provide daylight and views for the administrative and public spaces; a large crystal box containing the main lobby arises at the southeast end of the site. The facade, composed of structural louvers, retains a human scale and preserves the natural context for local residents despite the magnitude of the building.

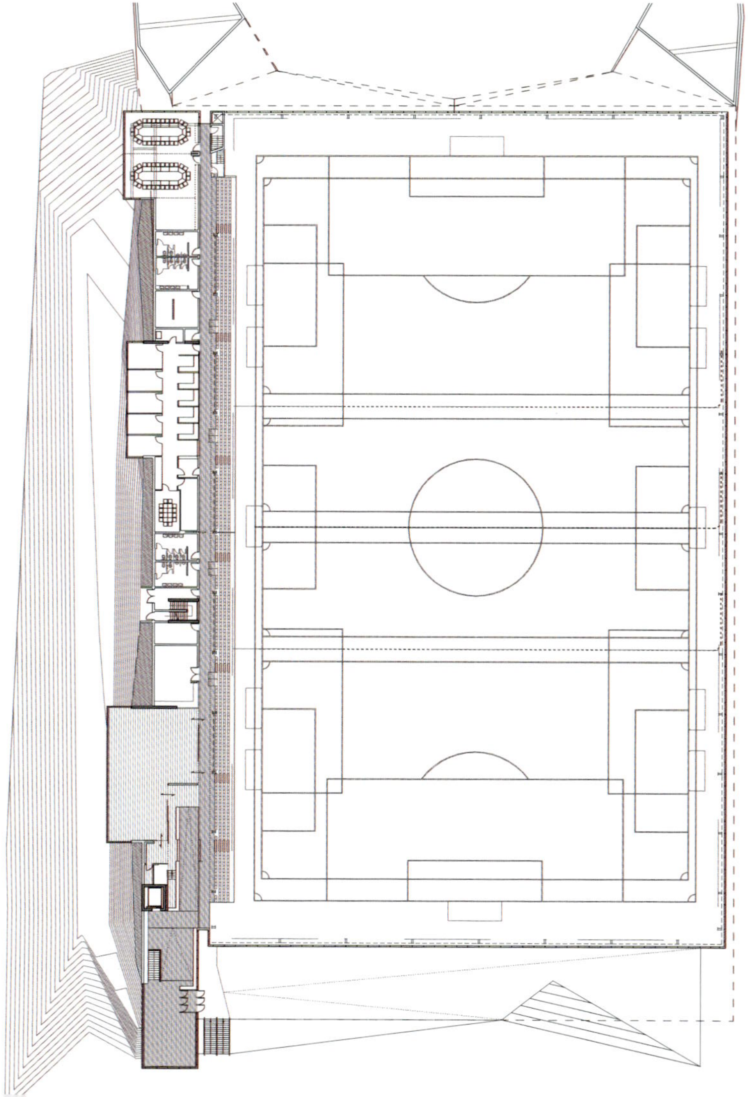

PLAN

COMPLEXE DE SOCCER

ROOF AXONOMETRIC

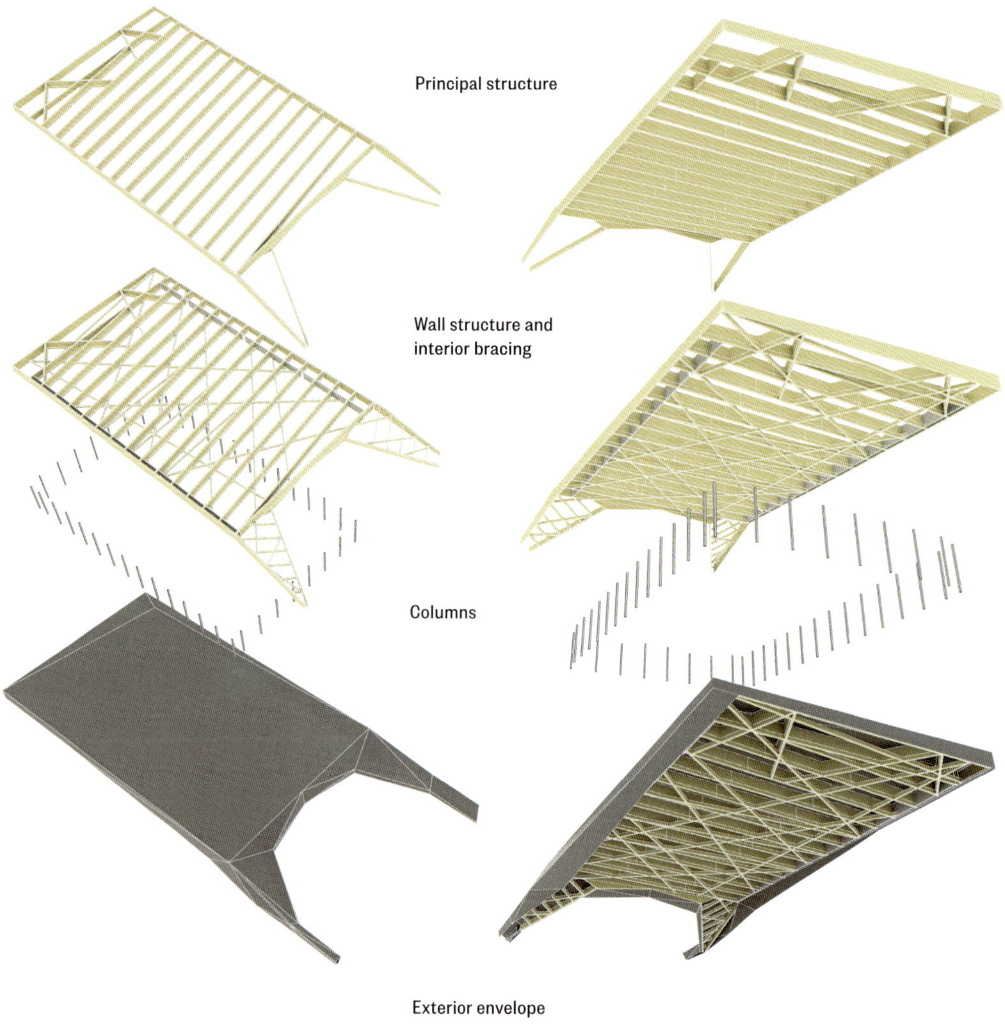

WORKS

Architecture Archive

Hugh Strange Architects

Somerset, England

2014

The Architecture Archive sits within a working Somerset farmyard at the foot of an agricultural valley. Nearby buildings include barns, wood storage, and outbuildings that date from the nineteenth century through the 1970s, as well as a recently completed cowshed. The project mixes simple construction techniques, prefabrication, and cheap industrial materials with high-quality, locally sourced hardwood to create a building that provides generous and luxurious interiors yet rests unpretentiously in its rustic environment.

The 120-square-meter structure was built within an old stone and brick barn. Some of the dilapidated walls were stabilized and restored; others were beyond repair and were removed, as was the roof. Two timber components were inserted into this framework atop a rough cast-in-place concrete base; a profiled cement roof, similar to those of the surrounding barns, extends the full length of the building to provide a covered entrance. Identical in volume, the timber forms are subtly differentiated through fenestration and interior fittings. The north building, an office space, is characterized by large French windows with views to the valley. The south building, a drawing archive and display area, is illuminated predominantly through generous skylights. To the rear of the building is a modest external space enclosed by a retaining wall; an external stair gives access to the surrounding woodlands.

The new building shell consists of a single layer of solid cross-laminated timber without insulation, external cladding, or internal lining. The spruce panels range in thickness from 300 to 420 millimeters and provide both insulation and thermal mass, creating stability of temperature and relative humidity for the drawing archive. A vented zone between the roof and the timber cladding prevents overheating during hot summer months.

In contrast to the engineered spruce of the CLT panels, the floors of the two volumes are fitted with hardwood "mats" of timber felled from the surrounding area and dried in the wood store. Rough-sawn cedar in the office and smooth-sanded and oiled ash and beech in the archive distinguish the two interiors. Specially commissioned display panels and curtains marry standard packing blankets with bespoke craftsmanship.

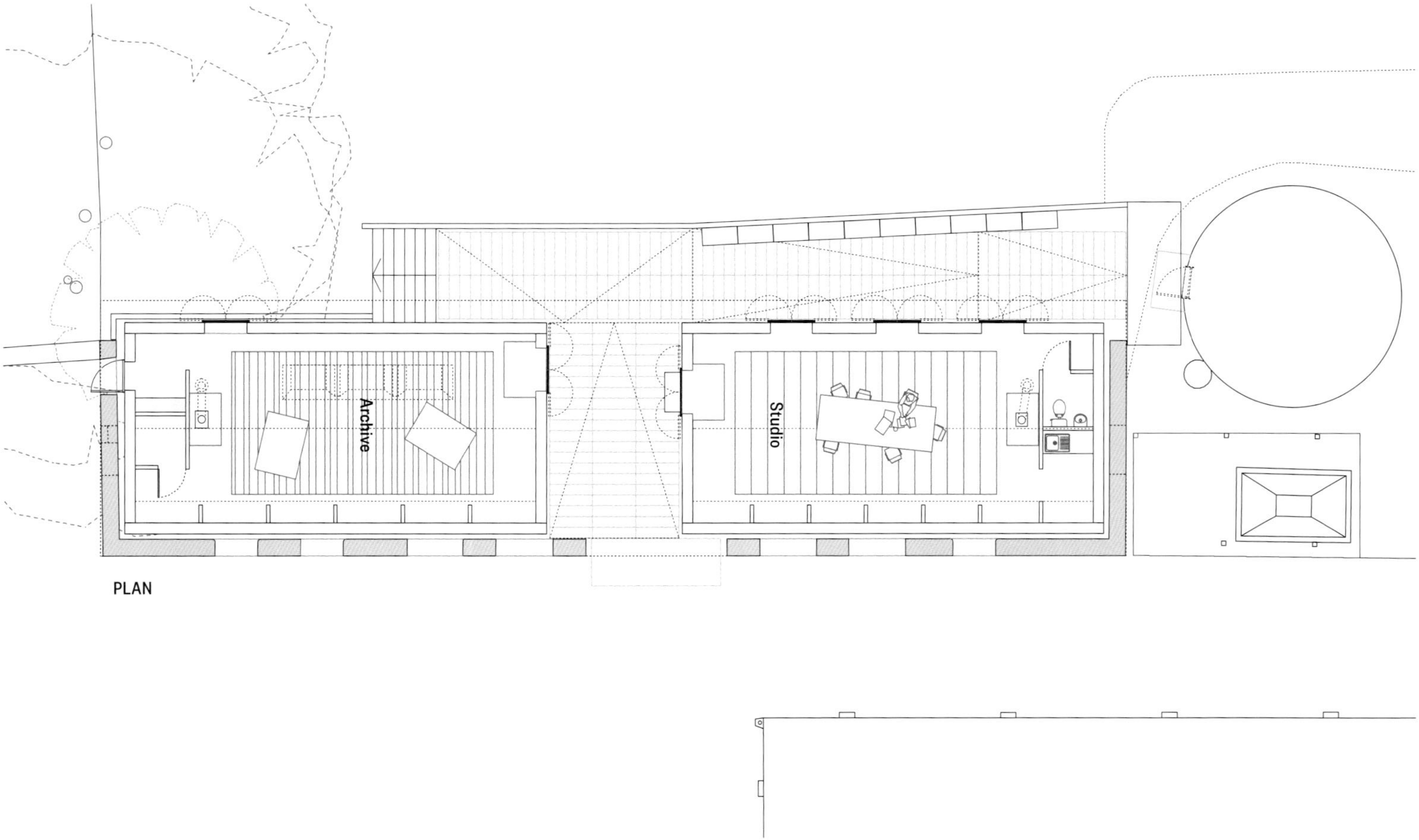

PLAN

AXONOMETRIC

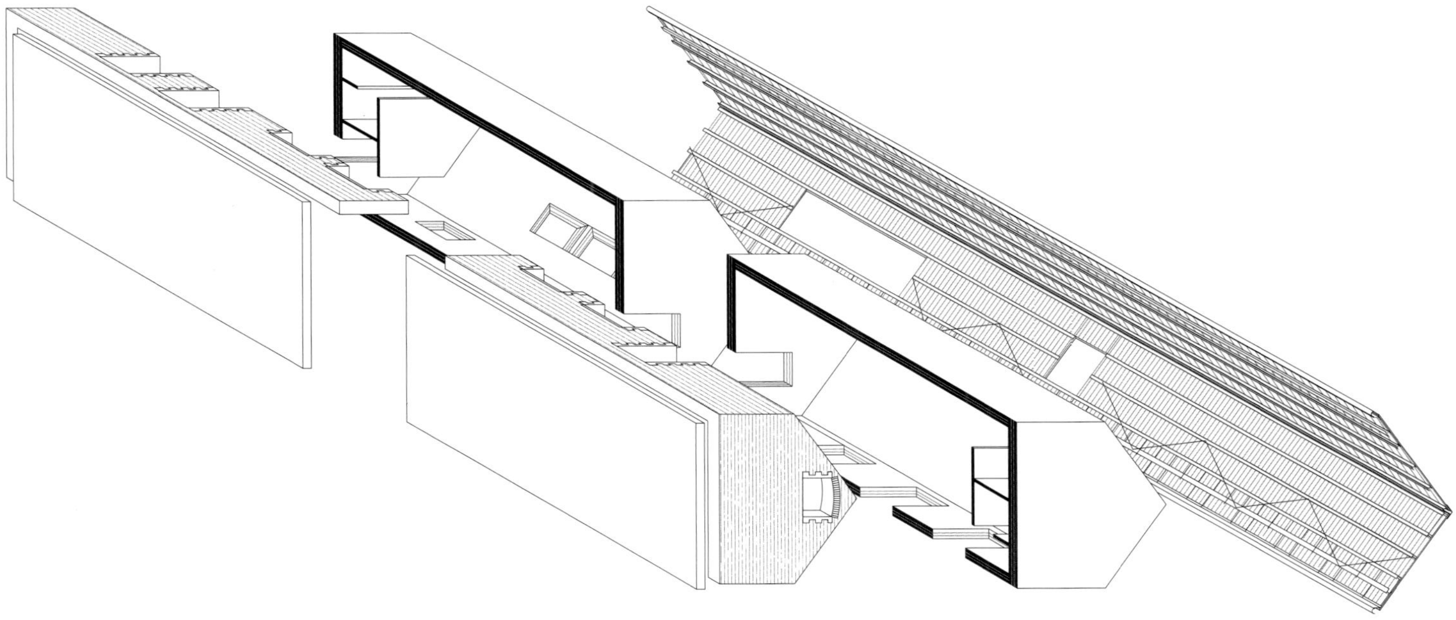

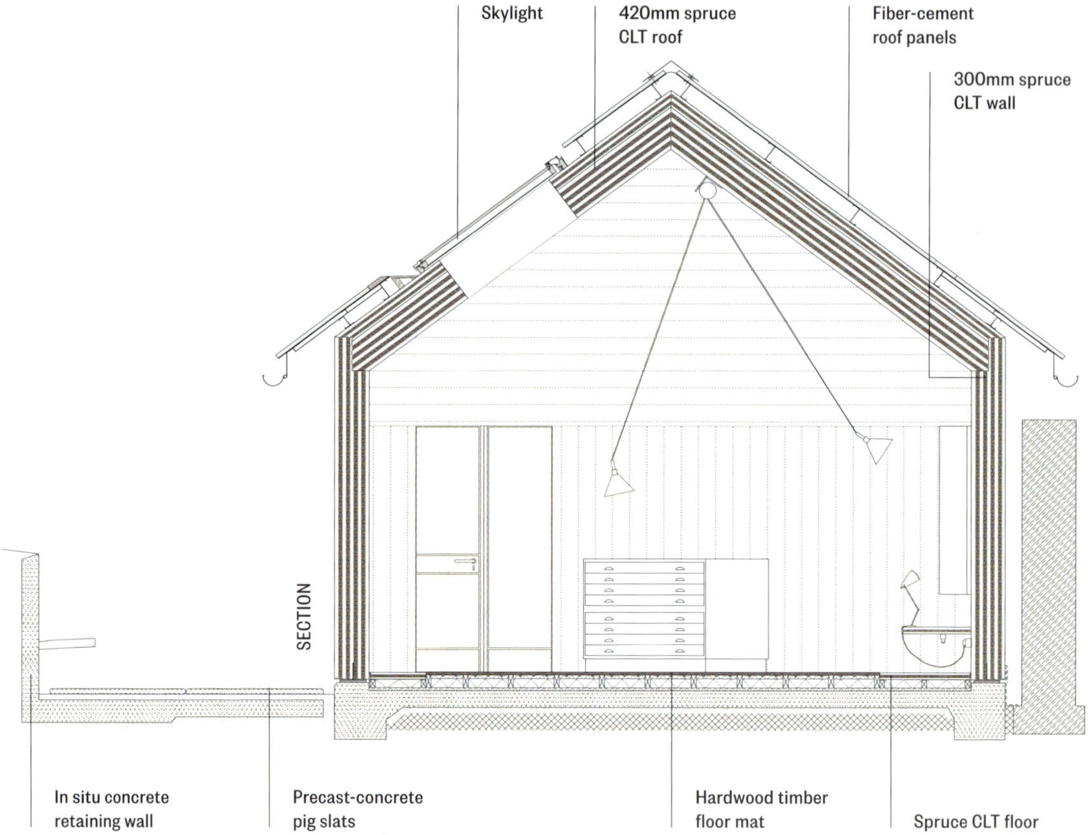
Skylight
420mm spruce CLT roof
Fiber-cement roof panels
300mm spruce CLT wall
SECTION
In situ concrete retaining wall
Precast-concrete pig slats
Hardwood timber floor mat
Spruce CLT floor

WORKS

Four Corners

Ultramoderne

Boston, Massachusetts

2014

The Four Corners pavilion reimagines the heavy timber bent in the context of contemporary mass timber technology to develop a new structural and spatial order. The project divides the traditional form of the gabled house into a series of rigid structural shapes made from cross-laminated timber. Employing a familiar figure toward unfamiliar ends, Four Corners creates unexpected spaces, structures, and avenues for a city transformed by timber construction.

The system is based on a series of column assemblages, each composed of four folded CLT "bents" cantilevered off a central spine. Though on its own each element is unstable, when multiplied the column assemblages create a matrix of interdependent structural trees balanced one against the next. The use of CLT enables long-span structures better suited to urban modes of inhabitation than to the agrarian types from which they spring.

The unity of space and structure in this configuration is a new phenomenon in timber construction. And where traditional bent-and-gable construction is characterized by a clearly contained form of a limited size, Four Corners voids the center of the form and turns the space outward. The resulting typology is a porous, and potentially limitless, structural mat of rooms, corridors, and courtyards in a spatial sequence that expresses itself through exploration.

As installed at the BSA Space in Boston, the pavilion is composed of three interlocking column assemblies that produce a network of corridors, courtyards, and outward-facing apses. The central courtyard area serves as a micro-exhibition space for a rotating series of video works. The corridors and apses lead to windows looking out to the city and use the architecture of the gallery to bring into being a series of semiprivate rooms.

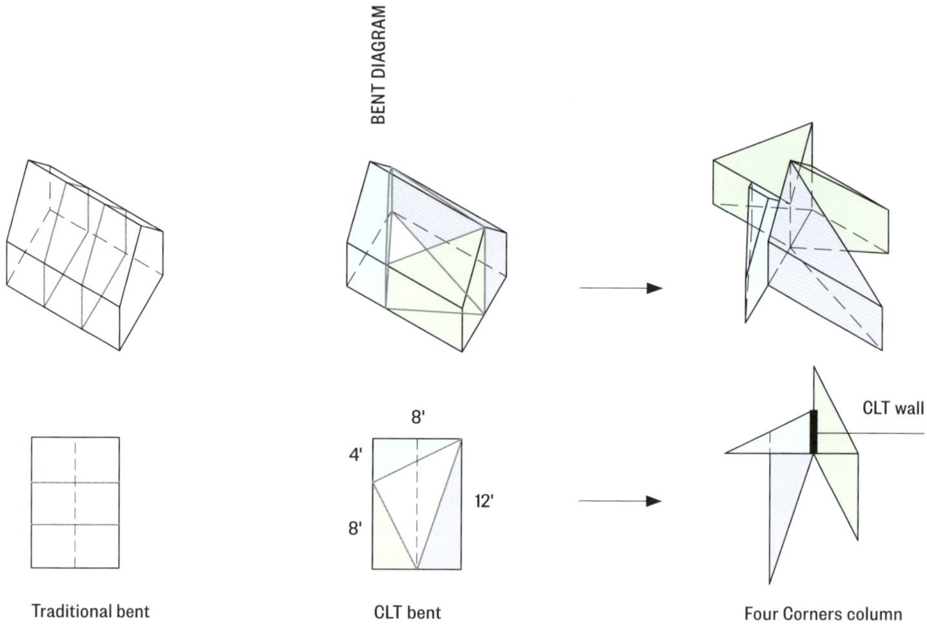
BENT DIAGRAM
8'
4'
12'
8'
CLT wall
Traditional bent
CLT bent
Four Corners column

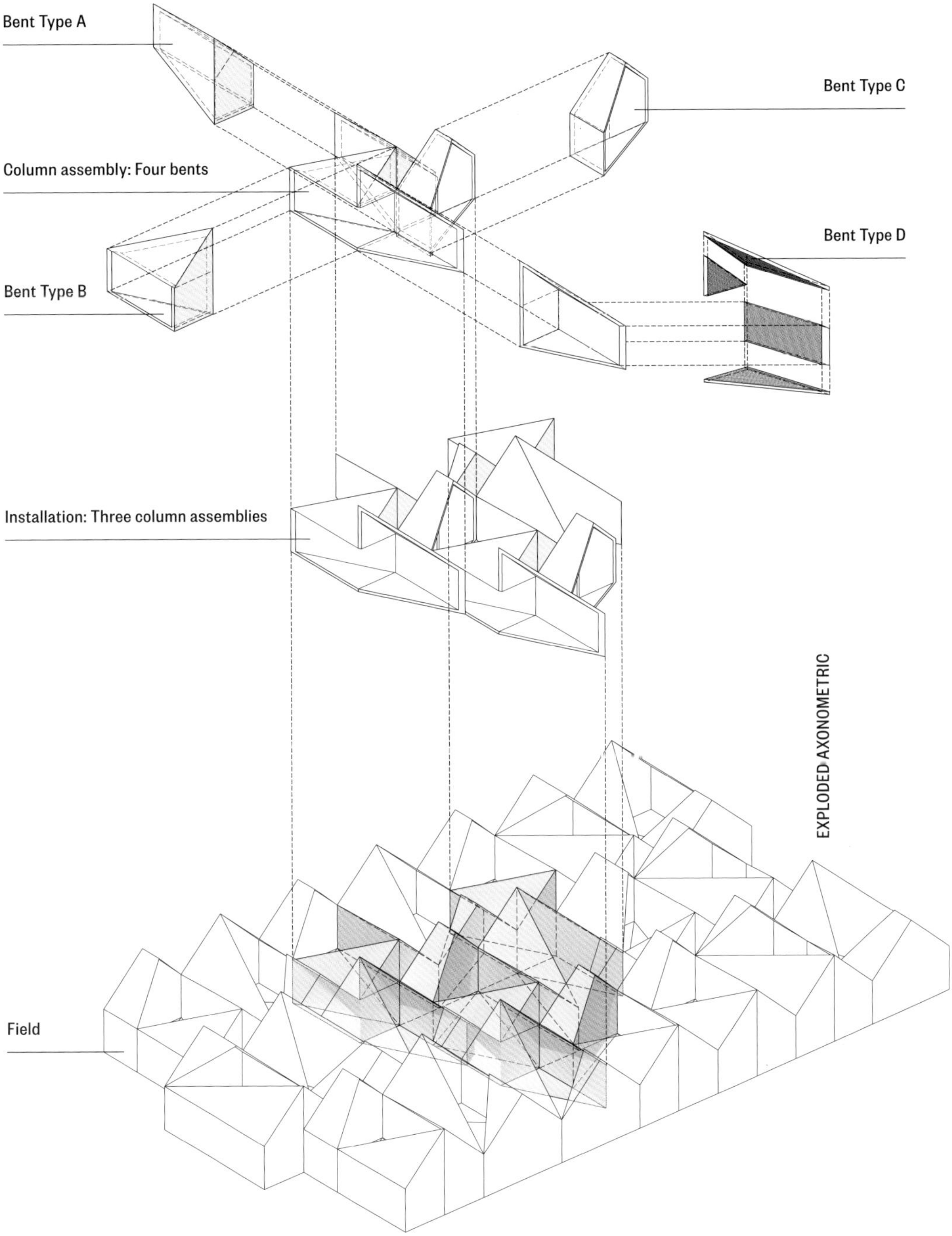

EXPLODED AXONOMETRIC

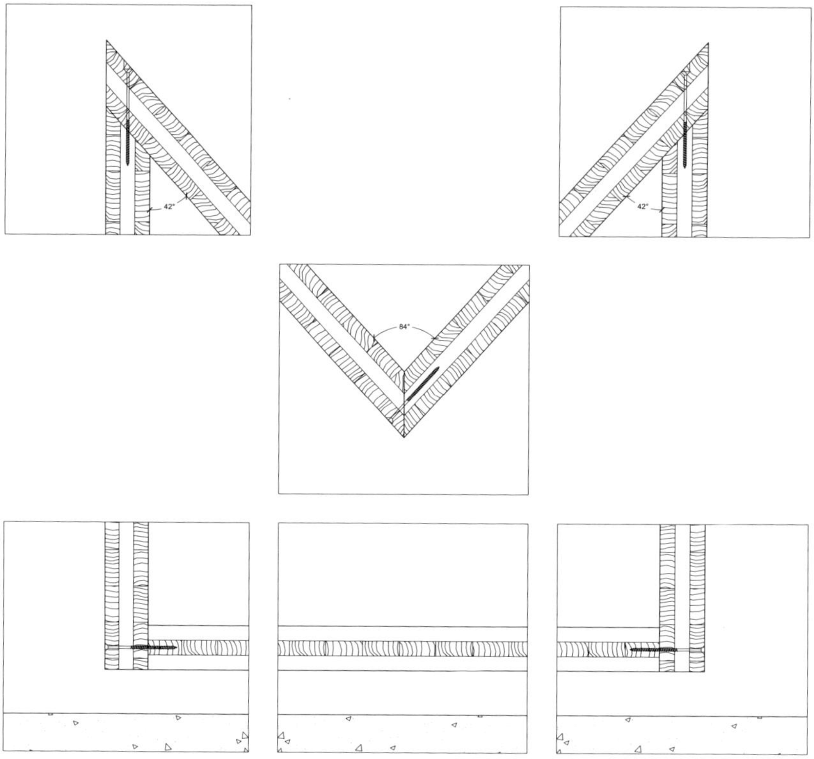

Section details at tunnel

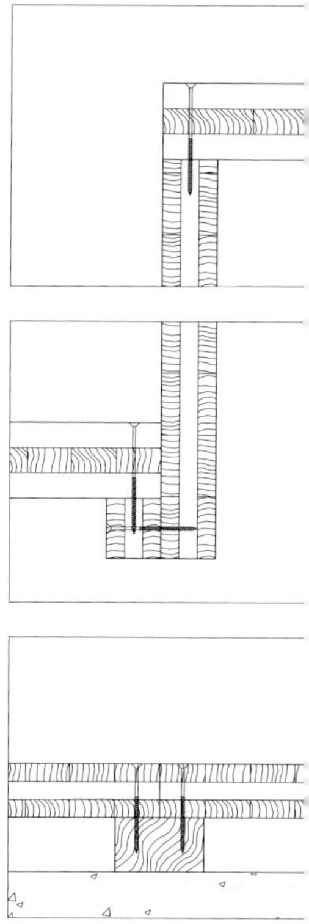

Section details at gable-to-gable connection

DETAILS

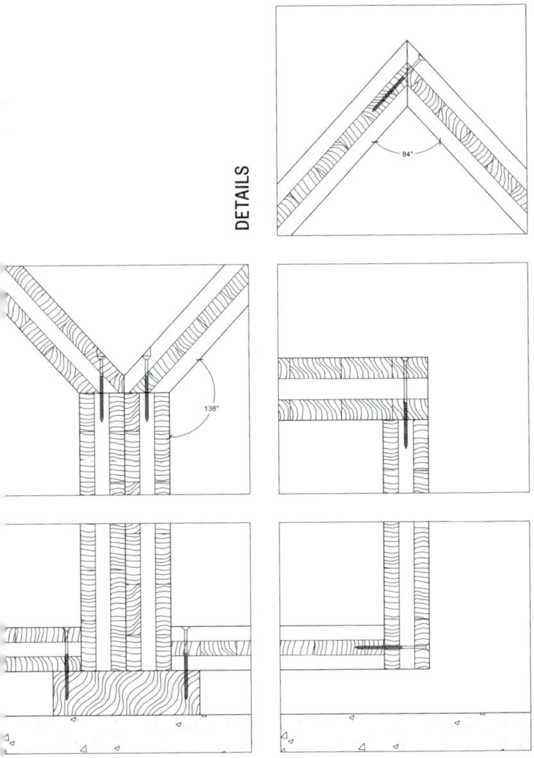

Section details at gabled bent

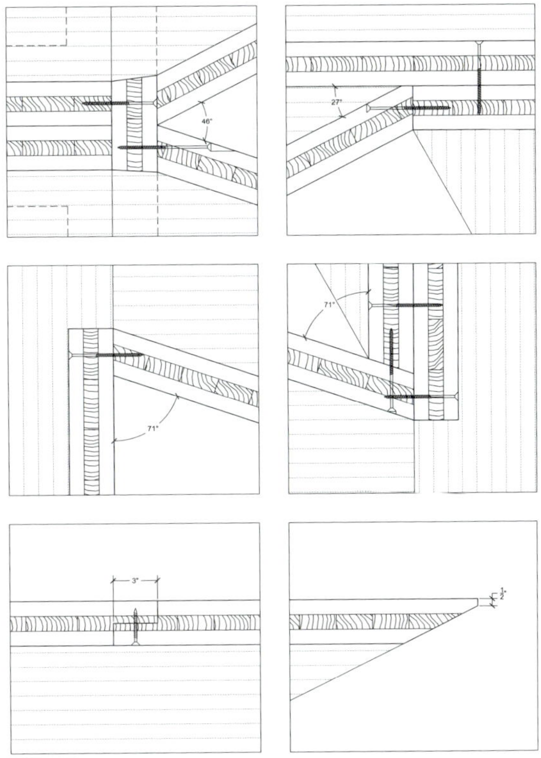

Plan details

Andrew Bernheimer is director of the Master of Architecture program and an assistant professor at Parsons The New School for Design. He is the principal of Bernheimer Architecture, based in Brooklyn, New York. Bernheimer was a founding partner of the award-winning firm Della Valle Bernheimer, subject of the monograph *Think/Make*. He has lectured at major universities and institutions, and his work has been featured in numerous articles and publications.

Illustration Credits

Olivier Blouin: 174–75 bottom
Didier Boy de la Tour: 108, 110, 114–15
Peter De Kan: 160, 162 top
Owen Detlor, High Performance Wood Seminar, Yale School of Architecture, Fall 2013: 20
David Grandorge: 178, 182 bottom, 183
Latreille Delage: 167 top
Nic Lehoux, Courtesy of Bullitt Foundation: 154, 156, 157 top, 158–59
Michael Moran, Courtesy of Otto Archive: 116, 120–21, 124–25
Norman A. Müller: 146, 148, 150, 153
Stefan Müller: 100, 102, 105, 106–7
Naturally:Wood: 136
Alan Organschi, TimberCity.org: 17, 19
Will Pryce: 29, 30–31, 40
Martin Tessler: 164, 169, 170–71